Ferny Wood

The Story of a Fallow Deer

Ferny Wood

Patricia Sibley

Whittles Publishing

Published by
Whittles Publishing,
Dunbeath Mains Cottages,
Dunbeath,
Caithness KW6 6EY,
Scotland, UK
www.whittlespublishing.com

Design by
Melissa Alaverdy

ISBN 1-904445-17-9

Printed in the UK by Bell and Bain Ltd

Contents

Preface

It all began with a telephone call from a stranger.

Robin Fletcher came for coffee, to pick my brains for his forthcoming broadcast in the 'Country Ways' series on the Isle of Wight. Two hours after that cup of coffee, we had decided to write a book together about the New Forest. Two months later, with the book having been commissioned, I was staying in Robin's cottage deep in the quiet part of the forest, encircled by woods. There, I was enchanted by the wildlife, the badger who came every night for supper, the birds, and most of all, the fallow deer. Robin was so used to them being around the old garden that he took little notice of them. But for me, coming from the Isle of Wight where there is little indigenous wildlife, they seemed so new and beautiful – and I fell in love with them.

Our book's story is built on a framework of long walks. Robin had been Head Forester until he took up professional wildlife photography instead and so knew the whole area like his own garden. We tramped its wild heathlands, explored bogs, rivers and villages and the ancient stands of oak and beech, for the Forest was actually only 'New' when planted by the order of Norman King William in the eleventh century. Everywhere we went there were deer, in spite of the Deer Removal Act enforced in 1851. At that time few had eluded capture, while others escaped from herds in private parks and slowly the numbers had built up again.

After our book was published I could not leave the deer, but spent every spare moment back in the Forest, watching red, sika and roe, but mostly my beautiful fallow. I studied them with very low-tech equipment: just binoculars, a pocket-sized notebook and a pencil. Zoologists claim that fallow deer were wiped out during the last Ice Age and reintroduced by the Romans for hunting. But I like to think that a few survived and bred, sheltered in our southern woods, so that they have roamed our land as true spirits of the trees for thousands of years.

I began to haunt a particular enclosure where fallow deer could almost always be found; let's call it Beech Grove. My companion on all these wanderings was George, my miniature long-haired dachshund; tiny, bad-tempered with strangers, but totally defensive of his Ma! (He even interposed his small, black and tan person between me and a doctor with a stethoscope!) Stubborn and wicked as most dachie puppies, he did unforgivable things such as chasing a mare and her foal and a litter of pigs, but gradually he learned to only go after rabbits and squirrels and to sit down at the sight of deer. His short legs never seemed to tire and I never felt threatened with his gallant person at my side. He was with me, leashed up, on that incredible early June evening which gave birth to this book.

Quite early in Beech Grove, I had sighted a small herd of fallow does and their young, browsing on newish leaves and moss. For hours we shadowed them through the wood, flitting from trunk to trunk, keeping them in view but never scaring them. Just before sunset, we had drawn quite close and hidden behind a massive beech bole. I peered carefully round it and there, only a few feet away, were half a dozen does in their bright summer colours – dappled with white – peacefully grazing with their fawns beside them. It felt such an honour to be accepted among them. Suddenly three things happened at the same time. One of the fawns, a sturdy little buck, turned and looked straight at me. A last low beam of sunlight shone right through the long-shadowed wood, spotlighting the fawn.

"Hello, little buck, hello Buckie," I said softly, then to etch this epiphany moment forever in my mind, a cuckoo called, loud and clear, close by. So I had to write about Buckie and followed him or his cousins all over the New Forest, watching them in all weathers interacting with each other or with wild creatures.

Many of my best sightings were thanks to George. One day, sitting on a fallen tree trunk and looking ahead to a row of old, dead hollies, hoping for a glimpse of a shy roe, I became aware that George, off the lead, had run back to my feet and was pointing, as only the long dachshund nose can, at the 'dead' branches. I realised, belatedly, that they were in fact a row of bare antlers! A herd of mature bucks were sitting with their backs to us, chewing the cud. Presently they stood up, stretched and ambled off up through the beeches. This was just such a herd as Buckie met beside the heath. Giving them a few minutes start, with George on his leash, we tracked them up through the wood to their evening feeding ground. Another day we had been creeping about that same wood for hours but had finally given up and were hurrying noisily homeward, striding crisply through the deep leaf litter, when George found a young roe all by himself and began to play with it, just as Buckie had tried to do.

A car makes a surprisingly good 'hide'. Some October evenings, we would take a supper picnic to the eastern woods, near the railway which Buckie followed, then wait for darkness to fall and the sika deer to appear. At dusk they would steal out of the pinewoods and often stand all around the car, uttering their spooky high-pitched mating calls, which had unnerved the young fallow deer. If George became too worried about the noises outside, another piece of sandwich would soon calm him down. Every November, it became a joke at home that 'Patricia had gone to the Forest for the rut!' and I did go, year after year, for this is such an exciting time in the deer world. Just to remember a great belching roar echoing out over the twilit, autumnal woods evokes a thrill of pleasure.

Perhaps it was fortunate that George, for once, was not with me in that evening dusk when I was charged by a tall-antlered buck, roaring wildly, eyes rolling with passion, though it sounds more dangerous than it was. His mind was not on me, but an errant doe. It was easy enough to slip safely behind a tree trunk and watch him chivvy her back towards the rutting floor deeper in the wood.

I had to watch, for after all, this represented the future of little Buckie…

Acknowledgments

My thanks to several keepers in the
New Forest who helped me with deer watching,
but prefer to remain anonymous.

The publishers would also like to thank Dr Jochen
Langbein of Consultancy Services for Wildlife
Research and Deer Management for his generous
assistance with manuscript proofreading and
suggestions for amendments to the text. Thanks also
to Dr Langbein for the provision of all the
photographs used in *Ferny Wood*.

Dedication

For my dear Jo Cookson,
faithful friend of many years,
ever since the ocarina!

1

Buckie's first dream

Summer sprawled over the great forest, lazy and warm. The buzzard gliding over Skythorns Ridge looked down on a vast green world, stretching from the rolling heathlands of Foxmoor to the dark conifers of Malwood, from the boggy hollows around Fiddley to the tall beeches of King's Ash. From the oldest oak in Amber Wood, a cuckoo was calling, although since it was now late June, he could only cry 'cuck-cuck'. The sound travelled far through the still air. Among the slim close-planted young beeches of Goat Plantation, a nuthatch gathered caterpillars to feed the last of his broods. Between wood and plantation, a grassy ride sloped down to the river in Amber Bottom and here the fallow deer were grazing. There were a dozen does and several yearlings, their dappled coats shining like copper with black tails whisking flies from white rumps. Now and then one would lift her head and freeze, tall-necked, ears forward, big dark eyes watchful, but she would soon relax and go back to grazing with the rest. Few people ventured deep into the forest, only the occasional visitor and the Keeper, with his labrador dog, Shadow. These last two the deer had learned to trust. The herd worked its way downhill, except for one doe who stood for a while as if deep in thought before finally sinking down in a patch of shade where bracken grew knee-high and the earliest of the heathers, cross-leaved heath, showed pink among its grey-green tufts of leaves.

Commoners' cattle, going down for a drink, had churned the river bank into a muddy slide after spring rains. Now it had dried rough and hard, though here and there a clearly set footprint was visible: a badger's paw, wide as that of a small bear; the three front toes of a crow; but mostly, prints of cloven hooves. The river ran clear brown, like good ale, under the arching trees, glinting where the sun could reach it through the heavy, mid-summer canopy and fast and shallow out in the middle. Near the banks it slowed into cloudy pools and a fallen twig might circle slowly among the pond-skaters. Swift winter floods had undermined the banks, exposing snaky ropes of twisted roots, scouring the earth bare in some places. Low water had left small crescents of gravelly beach. Three winters ago, in a violent storm, a branch had split off an ancient oak, planted by order of Charles II. It had fallen across the river and formed a dam where water suddenly splashed and babbled, breaking onto shiny ripples.

When the does had grazed down at the riverbank they turned aside, drifting silently away among the trees to lie down in the shade and chew their cud. Only one remained and this was a yearling. The male fawns of the previous summer had left their mothers in the early spring to wander and eventually join up with a buck herd. But the young does remained and this one turned her head on its slender neck to stare up the grass ride. Seeing her mother in the bracken, the youngster trotted back to nuzzle her ear, but the doe shook her head irritably, flicking her offspring away, for she was restless. The udder between her hind legs felt heavy and hot, dragging her down, yet she could not lie there in the cool grass by the river's babble like the rest of the herd. Presently, as if obeying instructions just received, she set off down the path and splashed through the stream, with the yearling following at a distance. Reaching the far bank, she turned eastward. Crossing spongy ground where pennywort grew like green leather buttons in the moss, she trotted onto Thorny Knap, slowed down and paused to lick at her flank.

Scots pines planted in close rows formed endless aisles of dark shade, the forest floor thickly carpeted with brown needles, yet even on this still day the higher branches still whispered and sighed together. Here and there, whole branches had fallen, leaving a scar that bled sticky gum. Some of this had hardened into silvery blobs that caught the meagre light like mirrors. Usually she felt secure among the pines, but today something was wrong. She lifted her head to filter the air with a wet, black nose, the yearling still shadowing her. Just inside the tree line to the north, lay the big hardened hummocks and holes of a badger's sett. A few discarded mats of old bracken lay about but no fresh earth, so it was not tenanted. The doe moved on, pain dragging deep inside her belly. Wood pigeons croo-crooed high in the branches and from one pine came a tiny high sound of the goldcrest. Soon the trees thinned out and she stopped, her nose flushing out an alien scent. Since she had last visited here, foresters had been at work. Sixteen ranks of trees had been felled, their stumps dabbed with a sea-green mixture to keep out the million spores of fungi that floated on the air. The lower boughs had been brashed and lay about the ground as cover for the next planting. The men had just gone home, up the gravel track in their dark green van. It was the exhaust fumes that the doe had smelt, even through the heavy reek of pine that hung over the felling.

By the forest was an old ruined cottage and Tom, who had once lived there, had let ponies and deer take over what was once lawn and geraniums. Old rambler roses, wild with freedom, had scrambled everywhere, so that buddleia, damson and apple trees alike bore cascades of crimson and white blossoms. All were filled with the deep-summer humming of the bees who lived in the cherry tree by the gate, where the doe loitered.

In front of the cottage walls lay Ivy's Lawn, a wide stretch of grass bounded by bracken and small hollies, the kind of cover that the doe instinctively sought. But today, a herd of heavy-bodied Friesians grazed it, dry cows from Buckherd who wandered up from their farm every morning and took themselves home again at night. Normally the doe would not have heeded them but now she stood hesitant under the old cherry tree that had lost a branch in the spring gales. Five years before, a young buck in the pride of his three-year antlers but driven mad by their peeling velvet, had thrashed them clean against the bole of this cherry tree and in doing so, had scraped off the bark all down one side. Since then, the northern branches had all died, having been starved of nutrient. Later that year, when wood mice had gathered all the cherry stones into secret hoards, the buck had served this waiting doe on his rutting ground in Thorny Knap.

As the cattle grazed steadily, moving away from her, the rhythmic munch-munch of the grass grew fainter, and half the lawn was now empty. The doe felt an urgent need to lie down and rest her hot, heavy belly somewhere dim and solitary. She took two small steps forward, head held high on her long neck, wet nose filtering the rich tide of scent: crushed grass, cattle slop, roses, rabbit, man and fox. Up in the north-west corner, inside the cover of holly and young oak, a vixen and her four cubs slept in their earth. The vixen had been out hunting that morning and had dragged home a fat rabbit. The cubs, three months old now, had thrown themselves on the carcase, worrying it and growling, boxing each other, rolling over and over, before finally tearing it apart and crunching up the bones. Though the smallest cub got the least, they were all comfortably full and tired out and lay curled up against each other. Around the tunnel entrance, their gambolling had flattened the bracken; all about on the stamped earth lay scraps of rabbit fur, bloody feathers and small, picked bones. Their father was out hunting.

The doe stepped back and looked round at the cottage walls with the paddock behind where she had always felt safe. Something moved within the doe and was pushed out under her tail as she trotted away into Ferny Wood. A brimstone butterfly flitted ahead of her through the sunny spaces as if leading the way. Ferny was no forester's wood but a sprawl of self-sown oaks, hollies and birches, the trees widely spaced on a gentle, southerly slope which was patched with foxgloves and bracken. In the grass grew lacy bedstraw and small, yellow flowers of tormentil. A thorn and two hollies, lapped with fern grew close together, the three trees were so closely hung about with ivy and honeysuckle bines that they seemed like one tree. Stepping through the bracken, the doe stood in a small triangular space, hidden away from the world of cattle and foresters. She lay down, her breath quickening. The bag had broken and she turned her head to lick at her wet hind legs and then stood up again. Two skinny hooves protruded from under her tail. Suddenly, in a slither of slime, a little buck fawn was thrust out, falling onto the grass. At once, his mother turned to lick him over, cleaning off the birth fluids, starting at the tail end. Slowly the wet brown colour began to dry out, revealing a rich chestnut with white dappled spots. Then the doe nosed beneath the fawn to make him stand. He gathered his long bony limbs together and tried to heave himself upright, but lapsed back into the grass – and so she nosed him again. This time he managed to stagger onto his small, pointed hooves then wobbled and fell over. On the third attempt he managed to stay upright although swaying slightly.

An old grey squirrel alone had seen the doe steal into her green tent. He used to live in a round drey in the top of a pine but now, wily and experienced in forest ways, he had taken over the more secure and sheltered residence in a woodpecker's hole, deserted the previous year. He had spent the morning swinging through the high branches, leaping lightly from tree to tree, chasing a female. Now he lay back in the sun where the tree forked to form a comfortable pouch, licking and grooming his pale belly fur and male parts with deep concentration. A hundred yards away the yearling grazed alone, where the grass grew especially lush around a fallen beech. None of the trees in Ferny Wood were very old, so this huge, upended root base must have been a relic of some former generation. Small ferns grew in the crevices of its north side, with cushions of star moss, while bracket fungus ate into the decaying wood, sending out its fan shapes in subtly striped greys and sepias.

The little buck was exploring his mother's furry flank, instinctively hunting for a teat and butting at her with frustration, in his newly-felt hunger. The doe tried to nuzzle him underneath her, spreading her back legs to encourage him. He was standing almost steady now, beautiful and new in the late afternoon sunshine. As the sun began its long descent north-westward, down the mid-summer sky behind the rise of Cuckoo Copse, the tawny owls of Malwood awoke and opened their great, round eyes. At the same time, the fawn found a hard ball between his mother's back legs and instinctively butted it. Seizing a teat he took his first delicious suck of warm milk and the doe soon felt the hot pressure in her swollen udder begin to cool away. When the fawn had drunk his fill, he lay down again, but his mother shook herself, feeling light, spry – and hungry.

Cautiously she stretched her neck above the fern, listening. Even the nuthatch was quiet and only a summer hum of insects filled the forest. Presently she stepped delicately out onto the path, the fawn tottering after her and crossing a patch of grass, led him into another stand of green bracken, its leaves still curled at the very tip. Knees already tired, the fawn sank down among the forest of green stalks. Feeling comfortably full he pressed his head against his small flank and fell instantly asleep, while his mother moved away through a stand of young pines. At their edge, she stood for a while, staring out across a green clearing. Nothing stirred so she moved on a little way and so was joined by her yearling, stepping soundlessly through the pines to graze beside her. Fat, yellow-brown puffballs grew in the turf. Later these would dry out and burst in a cloud of spores at the kick of a passing hoof. In damp hollows, lousewort showed pink and in places, a straggle of heath orchids faded into seed heads above their sinister-spotted leaves.

Suddenly the doe's head went up as she stretched high like a miniature giraffe, ears pricked forward, for a rumour of movement sweeping through the forest. The yearling looked up sharply too but in the end, neither of them moved. Some bucks came by at a swift trot, fifteen of them in all and close together. They held their antlers proudly high even though they were not yet fully grown and still in velvet, their black-edged tails switching across white, heart-shaped rumps and their chestnut backs double-dappled by leaf shadows moving over white splodges. The leading buck passed quite close to the little, sleeping fawn who could have been his son, sired in the long-gone, stormy, late-autumn days of the previous year. The fawn never moved as the hooves passed by although later, like a sleeping puppy, the fur of his blunt muzzle began to twitch as Buckie dreamed his first forest dream.

In the thicket beyond, a small brown bird began to sing, beginning with a few trills to tune up and then following with a cascade of song that lilted across Ferny Wood, pausing only when three more fallow bucks came galloping by. They were younger than those in the first herd, but were intent on catching them up. The nightingale sang on and on, proclaiming to the darkening world that this was his territory, for nearby, his mate brooded three skinny nestlings in a mossy cup-like nest among the hawthorn bushes.

Still the doe did not return. As slowly, the wind of the young bucks' passing died away the woods sank back into their summer evening silence and the dog fox from Ivy's Lawn came out onto the threshold of his earth, snuffing the cooling air, for he was hungry. He set off for the rabbit warren in Ferny Wood, passing a hundred yards north of Buckie in his bracken hide. Doe and yearling had grazed steadily away from the baby buck for his mother knew he would not need to be fed for another hour, at least. Keeper, on his homeward journey, paused for a moment, leaning on the enclosure gate beneath the cherry tree where the last bees were homing-in for the night. Sometimes on such warm, still evenings, the nightjars would begin their unearthly churr-churrings, but tonight all was still, the cottage ruins wrapped in the green mantle of the woods were silent.

When Keeper and Shadow had gone indoors at Marrowbones Lodge, three field mice scampered out of the garden and across the gravel track. They lived in a network of mouseways that they had tunnelled along under the cottage walls. In winter there were always fallen crumbs and nuts from the bird table and if they did not fall, the mice would run up after dark and fetch them. Tonight they found plenty of crumbs and stuffed them down, their eyes bulging. The biggest mouse, heavy with milk, had six blind babies to care for in a nest by the drainpipe so she was the first to scurry back. On the bank in Ferny Wood, young rabbits were out feeding and chasing and cuffing each other. Stealing up from behind, in the cover of some seedling pines, the fox smelled something different. As usual, deer scent lay everywhere which he never heeded, but there was something different about this scent. He stopped, one paw in the air, snuffing forward, pinpointing a clump of bracken three feet high. Buckie slept on, head tucked against his flank. Sometimes his eyes opened and he would delicately flex a small limb, but instinct told him to lie still under the curling fronds that filtered the greying air and smelled deliciously green. Full-grown fallow deer were far too large to be prey for foxes, but they would sometimes take a new-born fawn, although it was mostly skin and bones. Now, smelling fawn, the dog fox set out to cross the clearing and investigate, but just at that moment the ground began to vibrate with a drumming of hooves, so he stole under a holly to wait.

Commoners' ponies grazed all through his hunting grounds, but they did him no harm. This, however, was Keeper's daughter on her horse, trotting contentedly home. She helped her father to keep an eye on the forest ponies and paused now to check on a chestnut mare and colt grazing in a clearing. Startled, the colt dashed back to its mother and began to lick her shoulder with concentration. After a while the mare stopped grazing and turned her head to lick his rump but soon tiring of this, she began to move slowly away. But the colt headed her off, demanding attention and eventually she stood still, splayed her back legs slightly and let him suck for a moment before abruptly trotting off. When he tried to suckle again, she kicked out irritably and he took off at a gallop, small hooves drumming, ending up a hundred yards away where he began to graze young heather tops for himself. His coat was lighter than his mother's, thick and woolly-looking with a pale, six-inch mane, bunchy tail and big eyes with long dark lashes. Having watched this scene horse and rider moved on through the gathering dusk.

The fox meanwhile, had grown tired of waiting and had faded away into the darkness at the smell of human. He was not hungry, having already eaten half a fat rabbit. Now he ran off home with the other half held in his jaws, his head high, leaving drops of blood on the grass blades like a trail of small berries.

Doe and yearling stole out again when all was quiet. The doe, suddenly purposeful, moved back to the stand of bracken where the fawn lay and nudged him to his feet. He staggered for two steps but he was stronger now and soon found his balance. He reached for the udder now knowing where it was and settled to his supper, his small tail flicking to and fro with joy.

Out in the wider world it was Sunday, a day when thousands of people had poured into the forest, but probably not one in a hundred had even glimpsed a deer. Over in the east of the forest the sika deer kept to themselves. On western fringes, a herd of red stags were even now leaving the dark woods to spend the night grazing in a farm pasture. Wherever the cover was the thickest, the shyest of all the deer, the roe, lived their secret lives in family groups comprising father, mother and (usually), twin fawns. But the forest truly belonged to the fallow deer. They had moved lightly over it on their elegant hooves long before man's clumsy boots left their first prints, although the cruel ice had all but destroyed their herds, long ago.

When the little buck was comfortably full, he sank down into the bracken again. Summer night now lay over the land, cool and star-clear, and night creatures awoke and took over their kingdom. The boar badger from the huge old sett in Moonham Enclosure had been sleeping rough, away from home, ranging far out over Blackslade Bog to Golden Hat, where the ground stayed moist even in the summer drought. Wandering on down to Amber Bottom, he had dug out a nest of young rabbits and had spent the day in a small cave formed by the root cavity of an ancient, fallen beech, the winds of the previous winter having lined it comfortably with dead leaves. He stood just inside, sniffing the air with his blunt, black snout. Keeper had walked along the stream that morning but his scent was faint, so the badger padded out, heading through Ferny Wood for Moonham.

It was dark now with small rustlings in the fern and the bedstraw was a faint glimmer in the grass. Pale moths were in the air and far off, two branches creaked together making a weird sound in the night-time darkness. The doe, now grazing, heard the badger and raising her head, gave two quick barks, so deep and sharp that they might have been gunshots. It was a wild warning that made every fallow deer prick its ears for a moment and even woke the little buck from his sleep. But the badger, undisturbed, ambled on northwards, crossing Cuckoo Lane before coming out onto Ivy's Lawn, the starlight gleaming faintly on his white-streaked head. A host of rabbits shot back into their burrows there at his passing, drumming danger with their hind feet. The badger took no notice and neither did the tawny owl, perched motionless, a pale, still shape on the top bough of the cherry tree. For three nights now he had come to this perch, lured by the mouse scurryings below around the old walls. But for all his great round eyes and terrible talons, he would not venture too close to what had once been man's habitation. Below him the bees slept in their nest hole while a moth, attracted by the honey smell, flittered too close and was snapped up by the owl's hooked beak – hardly a mouthful. He gave up his vigil and leaning into the night air, sailed out over Ivy's Lawn emitting a long 'hoo-hoo-hoo' that seemed to set the darkness trembling and made the little buck shiver in the midst of his first dreams.

The dog fox heard that call, a mile away from the cherry tree while doing his nightly round of the small car park by Buckherd Lane – but he never paused. 'Take Your Litter Home', proclaimed the Forestry notice. At the foot of it, someone had recently thrown away a bag of chips that were still warm. Stuffed with rabbit, the fox was not really hungry but he ate one and then gathered up the bag in his narrow jaws and trotted back to his earth. Soon, scraps of greasy paper joined the detritus of rabbit fur and clean-picked bones that lay about among last year's litter around the earth.

With the first pale haze of light over the far-flung eastern heathlands, a cock crowed in the yard of Buckherd Farm and a blackbird whistled his first notes from the crab apple tree in Ferny Wood. As colour crept back into the forest, the fawn awoke to his first dawn. When his mother came softly through the bracken he stood up, tail end first, without having to be nudged. He could now stand firmly on all four spindly legs and he moved quickly to her udder.

The bees were the last of the forest creatures to awake since their nest faced westwards, away from first light. Years ago, a hole had been drummed by a woodpecker. As the tree slowly died and hollowed out, the bees had extended their galleries deep down inside the trunk. As the day warmed up, the first worker bee scouts flew out on their missions. By the time the sun had risen above the tallest pines in Moonham Enclosure, one had returned. On the comb within the cherry bole, she danced a kind of figure of eight, showing the watching workers how far to fly and in which direction. Soon they were flying out towards Ferny Wood, following delicate flight paths between bracken and birch, to a patch of tall foxgloves growing beside the resting place of the little buck. Two young squirrels, half-sized but fully furred, were hunting about in the clearing. Their brother, who had never thrived since birth, lay dead at the foot of a Scots pine. It was an odd-looking tree for it had once been topped by a browsing fallow buck and now, a mere twenty feet high, it bore a bushy top, just right for a squirrel's drey. Presently, rabbits came out to graze. Tits twittered overhead, gathering beakfuls of slim, green, moth caterpillars.

Keeper, accompanied by Shadow, left his lodge to make his early rounds, noting little orange and brown gatekeeper butterflies on the bramble leaves and half a dozen silver-washed fritillaries with their glowing amber-speckled-with-chocolate colours. They were feeding on the first bramble flowers, with their fragile pink cups resembling tiny dog-roses. Sadly, there was only one white admiral butterfly to be seen. In old books it was noted that these were once so plentiful in the forest that when the sun came out, they would drift down from the oak trees like falling snow. Over-planting of conifers in the forest had shaded out the honeysuckle on which their caterpillars fed, and those plants that had survived were eaten by ponies or deer. Keeper followed a yellow brimstone butterfly into the sunny spaces of Ferny Wood. He thought that it was probably searching for a buckthorn on which to lay its eggs as he made for a patch of brambles above the rabbit bank. Here, a whole cloud of little, dark-brown ringlet butterflies were browsing on the flowers. Keeper sat down with his back against an oak tree and, taking out a small notebook, recorded the butterflies that he had seen. Then he put it away and just for a moment, let the life of the woodland wash around him in a green tide, birdsong and leaf dapple, insect hum and flittering wings. Shadow fell asleep. In a distant clearing a fallow doe grazed. She was rather small and probably a yearling. A bee zoomed past Keeper's left ear and a scent of crushed bracken eddied on the light morning breeze. Foraging bees from the cherry tree were busy pillaging pollen from the tall stand of purple foxgloves, just where the fawn lay, still hidden in the fern. When a bee flew too close, he twitched an ear and Keeper caught the slight movement.

Dropping to his knees, he parted the bracken very slowly and gently and found himself a foot away from the newborn fawn. He knelt there for a long moment, struck dumb with wonder at this little creature, so beautiful and small and still. He had never been so close to such a young deer before not during all his years in the Forest. Presently he said softly "Hello then, little Buckie," and drew the leaves together again, hiding the fawn from view.

At this time of the year, anxious visitors to the Forest would often come to his lodge or ring up to report 'an abandoned baby deer' that they thought they had found. "Leave it alone, go quietly away and its mother will come back to feed it", was his constant advice. So on this occasion he and the dog stole homeward, though he would always remember that bonny little chestnut body, all dappled with white. Neither would he forget the pale, stick-like folded limbs ending in neat dark hooves, nor the broad head with its short, puppy-like muzzle, the wide space between the black, almond-shaped eyes, the pointed ears laid back along its neck – and the wet, black nose.

When, at last, there was shade under oak and thorn, the doe walked back to her fawn, ambling along the grassy rise, pausing to graze now and then. Though Keeper and Shadow had long gone, she smelled them on the fern and let out two gunshot barks, bringing Buckie to his feet with a sudden sense of urgency. He scrambled upright and stepped toward her, making for her udder. But she moved away a few paces and turned her head, waiting for him to follow. So Buckie took his first walk before being nosed firmly into another bank of fern some ten yards away. While he suckled, his mother gave him a thorough licking over, starting with his rump and tail, and then moving up his spinal ridge. When he had finished sucking, she finished off with his ears, cleaning them inside and out. Even then, she stayed with him for longer than usual before moving away to graze again, the yearling materialising from nowhere to follow her like a shadow.

For a few more days, Buckie dreamed the hours away in his green, bracken world –then he woke to the forest and all its joys. That morning, after his breakfast milk, he leapt into the air on all four feet, just for the fun of it, surprising himself. Tides of scent washed against his nostrils, demanding to be investigated. There was crushed grass and rabbit, bedstraw and bank vole, human, squirrel, pony dung and gorse bloom. Tall ears twitching forwards registered a tap-tapping high in an oak tree where a nuthatch was working the bark for insects. There was the sound of ponies wrenching off grass, the hum of bees and a thousand small rustles in the grass, all around. When his mother moved off he trotted after her with a stiff gait, like a clockwork toy just wound up.

One July morning, he watched his mother lower her head and begin to graze in a clearing under the light leaves of a birch. After a moment he tried to do the same, tearing off a small mouthful of grass with his milk teeth against his hard palate, lifting his head to chew. Most of the grass fell out again, but the green taste was new and exciting, like everything in this woodland world. He was so intoxicated with it all that he galloped three times round his mother, before collapsing back onto the ground, his long limbs folding up suddenly. August brought other creatures into his world, even to the quiet glades of Ferny Wood. There were picnickers, walkers and pony-club riders from the nearest stables. Once more, the doe began to feel restless, threatened by all this activity. So one evening, as the first stars brought a breath of cooler air to the sultry woods, she stood still for a long time under the birches, tall-necked, turning her head slowly east, then west, snuffing the twilight. Presently she set off southwards at a brisk trot, the yearling close beside her, looking back from time to time to see that her fawn was following. The dog fox from Ivy's Lawn was on his way to the rabbit warren. He felt a small vibration in the ground as the deer trotted by, and though he smelled fawn, he turned away. Whatever dangers lurked in the forest, and they were many, Buckie was now too big to make a fox's supper.

Deeper and deeper into the woods they moved, where the trees grew taller and closer together. Here, their hooves crisped through old leaf litter rather than soft grass. By the time the tawny owls screamed out from Moonham Pines, Buckie, for the first time in his small life, felt tired and hungry. After all, he had never walked so far before or knew his world to be so big. At last, under the great oaks of Amber Bottom, they paused and he seized the opportunity to take a quick suck.

From across the stream came a single deep bark – it was time for Buckie to join the herd.

2

Galloping Hooves

At first light, Buckie and his mother splashed across the shallow-running Amber Brook into Goatshorn and ambling between the young beeches paused now and then to browse leaves from a low bough. They startled a wren into making his tic-tac call that sounded all through the valley, where mist still hung in fading wisps above the river. The doe stood still allowing Buckie to suck, turning her head to lick over his tail and rump. Then they moved out onto the wide grassy ride between the young plantation and ancient wood, where the fallow deer herd had lingered at mid-summer. Since then, it had divided into smaller groups as the does left to bear their young. Higher up the ride there grazed a small family, a menil doe with her yearling and fawn along with another doe who had not bred that year. The menil's coat was lighter than that of the rest – a deep gold dappled with white but with no black line on her whisking tail. Her fawn, some days older than Buckie, stood stocky and strong with a pale coat like that of his mother. The other doe, whose coat was of the common colour, walked on three legs. Last October, while being chivvied across Marrowbones Lane at twilight by a groaning buck, she narrowly escaped death beneath the wheels of Keeper's Landrover. He had jammed on the brakes but had still struck her a glancing blow with the bumper. For hours he had searched for her by torchlight and with the aid of Shadow the labrador, but he had not found her that night. In fact, only her lower left foreleg was injured, being broken below the knee. The bones never really knitted back together and so she had learned to hold the lower part of her leg at right angles to the ground and walk on three legs. She had not been able to stand for her pursuing buck and so this summer, she had been a kind of aunt-doe, staying with the menil and her fawn, sometimes grooming the baby and keeping watch.

As Buckie and his mother grazed up the ride, a third fallow deer stole out of the plantation to join them and this was the yearling that had never been far away. Buckie was trying to graze properly now, mostly on grass but also on wild strawberry leaves, dandelions and a leaf or two of woodsage. Soon the two families intermingled and later, when Buckie's mother moved away into Amber Great Wood, the others followed her at intervals, until all seven deer were lying together. They lay, chewing the cud under the boughs of a vast spreading oak that had once been pollarded and was now home to hundreds of forest creatures. While the deer ruminated, a tree creeper crept up the bole of the tree, probing the cracks with his thin curved beak. Halfway up, he flew back to the ground, landing beside Buckie, before starting upwards again. Then the lame doe suddenly stretched her neck, with her ears high and forward. Next she stood up, staring downhill towards the stream. Raising hind legs first, the rest then stood up and moved closer together, all looking the same way. They sniffed the air and the does glanced round to see that their fawns were close by. Obviously smelling alien scent, they wheeled about and with a quick flash of white rumps they vanished, leaving only the faint print of their bodies on dry oak leaves, compacted together.

Keeper had seen them though and had been viewing them for five minutes, leaning against a beech bole with the light breeze in his face. Shadow lay motionless at his feet. Ever since her puppyhood, she had known that raised binoculars meant 'freeze'. Keeper noted that another doe and fawn had joined the menil family. Watching them stand up he had seen the lame one stagger. "Best be shot in the September cull," he thought, although usually only the bucks were taken then. But the doe would never be able to cope with a hard winter. She might even be the one he had hit with the Landrover. "There are some good strong fawns coming along, though," he mused.

"Go on then," he said to Shadow. She shot away and tore round in circles, sending every squirrel in sight up the nearest tree though none would scamper far. One sat on an oak bough above her head, swearing with a sound like hard kisses.

Keeper paused for a breather, just in time to see a fallow buck saunter across the ride below, tall-antlered, and with head held high. He watched for a time, but no other deer came. The herds were already breaking up then, a sign that the old magic was at work. Shadow eventually reappeared at his side, content to potter along near him. Buckie's mother had heard the dog commotion and had looked up once, but had then returned to her grazing. The little group had not run far when Keeper passed, and soon returned to their couches under the oak. All through August it was the place that they came back to most often and they were soon joined by a black doe and her yearling.

The two fawns were the first to stand and ambled along side by side for a few yards until the elder suddenly skipped into the air, did a quick turn, lowered his head and butted Buckie's flank. Buckie was two feet tall now and losing his fragile, baby look; his muzzle was lengthening, his neck was beginning to thicken and he was becoming strong. He whipped around and lowered his head to charge the other fawn. Their bare, furry foreheads met, bracing against each other, a forerunner of a future day when they might clash great antlers. Shoving hard, first it was Buckie that gained ground and then his opponent, until they broke apart and stared at each other with bright black eyes. Then Buckie, obviously aware of a wild new strength flowing through him, reared up, pawing the air and set off at a gallop around the oak tree's mossy trunk. Round and round the pair went, until the little owl, watching from above, did a double bob and screamed twice before gliding away on its pale, rounded wings to find some quieter mouse-ground.

Most September evenings, as the first leaves began to drift down in Amber Great Wood and the days shortened, the little bucks would play, sometimes with the yearlings joining in. Once, they were interrupted. Silently, out of the darkening spaces between beech and oak, there stepped a huge, old buck, his majestic antlers towering over the does that turned to stare at him. The fawns froze in their game, like naughty children sighting the Headmaster. The buck stared back at them, motionless, then he gave a grunting, guttural bark, pawed at the deep leaf litter with one hoof and moved away, muzzle high and proud to balance the great spread of antlers.

Hence, when shots rang out through Amber Bottom and the marksmen came for the lame doe, the group had vanished away. They were hidden in the deep gloom of Moonham Enclosure among the close-planted pines that stretched eastwards, acre upon acre in endless dim aisles of brown twilight, even on a sunny noon. They had not followed the old buck, but his visit had spread restlessness among the does. That night after his visit, they had not wandered out to graze the rides of Amber Great Wood under the harvest moon, but had moved eastwards along Amber Brook to the gentle slope of Hogshades, where acorns were beginning to splatter on the first fallen leaves.

Nearly a mile away, up in the eastern corner of the vast Enclosure, there was a rutting ground, but the group moved westwards through the dark, needle-carpeted avenues, towards Ivy's Lawn. Apparently drunk with all the space, after the close-planted trunks of Moonham, Buckie threw himself into the air stiff-legged, like a wooden toy on springs. Pronking was the word Keeper used for this behaviour – but the does grazed on, unconcerned. When the sow badger returned with a bundle of fading bracken clasped against her chest, she skirted around the grassy space to avoid flying hooves and scuttled backwards down into her sett in the copse. Its floor was striped black and white with moonlight and tree shadow. Soon she was back out for supper. A recent shower had brought up a crop of fungus at the copse's edge and a host of long, dark-brown slugs had crawled out to feast on them. She gulped down the succulent slugs, her small eyes gleaming.

Buckie's mother was also having a change of diet. Grazing along the southern edge of the wide stretch of grass, she had come upon the first fallen crab apples, deep-bedded in the grass, orange and russet. The fallow deer lingered near Cuckoo Copse and gorged with fruit, they rested under the young oaks and birches. The lame doe groomed Buckie's neck and ears, running the fur lightly between her teeth. He flicked off flies with his tail while his mother lazily scratched a tick from her ear. Overhead, two squirrels reached for the same acorn and the younger one's paw grabbed it first. But the older male shot after him and the two swung through the upper branches, leaping and scolding, making enough noise for a troupe of monkeys, shaking the high boughs so that a storm of leaves and nuts pattered down on the woodland floor. But the fallow deer never even glanced up and soon the commotion died away over Malwood. Buckie's head drooped lower and presently he slept, his head curved round on his flank, while his yearling half-sister ruminated, her jaw moving in a slow, regular rhythm. Clouds hung low over the forest and the air was grey with moisture, slicking grass and leaves with a damp film and condensing on Buckie's eyelashes.

When a car drove down Cuckoo Lane, the deer took little notice as they were used to Forestry vans and trailers passing, their drivers stopping to unlock the padlock on the five-barred gate. The young driver of this car didn't know about the padlock and he had imagined that he could drive his girl deep into the woods where they could make love in peace. Confronted with the gate, he swore and turned the car round so roughly that it skidded on the gravel. But the girl put a hand on his arm.

"Hey, let's stop for a minute. We might as well give Skippy a run, now we're off the road." He stopped the car, although a run was not what he had in mind. The dog was a Jack Russell terrier, bursting with a hunter's energy, nine months old and totally undisciplined.

"Come on, Skippy." Even before the girl had said his name, the terrier had shot from the car and out onto the splendid freedom of Ivy's Lawn. He tore round in a circle, stopping only to lift a leg and then was off like a bullet into Cuckoo Copse, yelping madly.

"Skippy! Skippy!" yelled the girl as he disappeared from sight through the fringing bracken.

The deer were already on their feet, Buckie's mother being the first to start up. At first sight of this black and white barking thing, they leapt away through the straggle of trees. To veer east would bring them back onto the exposed lawn and westwards, the girl was running along the track, calling crossly. So the deer could only turn north toward the road. Skippy tore after them, scarcely touching the ground or so it seemed, his eyes rolling, a hunter at last. Buckie was scared as he had never been chased before and kept close to his mother's flank. When they burst out of the copse onto Buckenhead Lane, the deer were in a tight group, all except for the lame doe who couldn't keep up. As they careered across the narrow road, a van driver slowed to watch them gallop away over the heath. "Beautiful sight", he thought, "not often you see them so close". He put speed on again, taking eyes off the road for a fraction of a second for a last sight of their fleeing white rumps. When the lame doe suddenly appeared right in front of him, she had no chance at all. At least she was killed instantly. He got out, white-faced.

Then a small, rough-coated terrier appeared, panting, wild eyes, tongue lolling. "Your fault, you bloody dog. Look what you've done!" he shouted. It sniffed at the dappled gold carcase and slunk away.

The deer had galloped far out across the heathland but Buckie began to fall behind, bleating with fear – a tiny sound in this immense landscape. The does and yearlings slowed down and milled about for a moment, then they stood still, close together, staring back the way they had come with their necks stretched tall and ears high. Buckie stumbled up to his mother and nervously tried to suckle, his small tail arching over his back.

Under a lowering sky, Foxmoor Heath stretched away on every side, the ridge of Skythorne to the north forming its only visible boundary. Acres of very old ling bushes, three feet high, gave way to tawny bracken, patches of seedling pines or wet hollows fringed with yellowing rushes, although the grey air seemed to suck all colour from the bleak landscape. Yet in scattered nooks over the heath, south-facing banks still bore small, purple scabious, sprouts of gold ragwort, even sprigs of cross-leaved heath, still showing pink. Far away a hen harrier slid round a circle of air on his black-tipped wings, hinting pipits. The does made half-hearted efforts to pick at sere mats of grass, while drifting on westwards. They grazed through a small stand of birch, then found themselves on the banks of a pool, shining with a steely light. Like most of the forest ponds, Foxmoor Pool was an old, flooded, gravel pit, now with grass covering its banks and small pines and willows clothing the two islands out in the middle. Fishermen came sometimes, but no one was there that evening, only a mallard cruising offshore and a white glimpse of swans between the islands. The deer stood, ears pricked forwards, suspicious in this strange place bare of cover. But the grass grew lush and green here and soon the black doe had lowered her head and begun to graze.

Buckie tucked in too, he could graze perfectly well now and had only sought his mother's udder for comfort. Then they sat for a while under the pondside birches, until one by one, they stood up, staring out into the wild, bare spaces of the heath and taking a few restless steps forwards or sideways. Eventually, they were all facing one way and then with his mother in front and Buckie following closely behind, the group began to move slowly southwards back towards the woods. They paused often, stretching their necks and trying the air. All this country was strange with no familiar scents and the deer felt an urge to leave this alien territory behind. Ahead, there was an occasional roar and flash of lights in the darkening air, but when, at last, they came to the road, it was clear of traffic. A brief hardness beneath their hooves and then the heath was left behind and the little herd broke into a trot across the wide green verge, seeing that they were back in the familiar ground of Cuckoo Copse.

Rain poured down all night while they huddled under the thickest hollies. In the darkest hour, two bucks came sauntering down the track side by side and a shiver of excitement swept through the does. As the bucks disappeared across Ivy's Lawn, the black doe made a half-hearted attempt to follow, running out onto the grass and blinking the heavy rain from her long lashes, before turning back into shelter. By dawn, the clouds had rolled away eastwards and soon pale sunshine swept across the Forest. It was like a great gold brush painting in colour after colour, orange berries on dark hollies, brilliant yellow horse-chestnut leaves patterning the ground, bracken fading from a wan green to yellow and sepia and cherry leaves turning crimson around the bees' nest. Only a few birch leaves had changed colour as yet, as if a shower of gold fell lightly down through their lacy green branches.

Later in the day, under the castellated walls of a mock-castle, horses teetered down from their boxes and hounds milled about, their tongues lolling and tails agog. Eventually, they chased a fox away to the north through Yew Tree Moor, only to lose him in the far distant thickets of Rushy Bottom. So it was not the hunt's galloping and hallooing that made the fallow does restless. As darkness gathered under the hollies, they moved out onto Ivy's Lawn under a sky bright with cold stars. For a while they stood clear of the copse, the menil doe with her yearling and fawn and Buckie with his mother and sister. Then, as if some secret signal had passed, they set off together across the squelchy grass, making for the scrape under the fence that led into Thorny Knap. The pinewood smelled resinous and cold. They flitted fast through the close, dark aisles, silent as shadows on the thick carpet of dead needles. Coming out of the dense trees, Buckie paused to graze the succulent shaded grass of the verge, but the rest did not stop. They ran on eastwards as the three stars of Orion's Belt rose in the sky, so that in the end he had to gallop to catch up with them again, barging into the menil fawn, wanting him to play. In the short time that he had been away, more does had joined the herd. Now the pace quickened, running downhill over Amber Brook and then uphill to country Buckie had never seen before. A strange grunting cough sounded across the dark slope and a rank smell hung heavy on the air. They followed a track already scored by dozens of neat hoof marks into Hogshades, an old oak wood facing south-west, the trees wide-spaced with clumps of seedling pines scattered here and there.

Halfway up the steep slope, last year's leaves had been churned into black mud that was laced with urine and round the edge, frayed stumps glimmered in the darkness, like small albino animals, watching. More does stole out from the higher ground and the air shivered with excitement. But the rutting ground meant nothing to Buckie; that year it was just a dull stretch of ground offering nothing to eat. For comfort, he fumbled towards his mother's udder, but she shifted irritably away. Close at hand came a clashing of antlers and grunting, the sound of an animal blundering away. Then the master buck stepped out and stood proud and alone in the middle of the rutting ground, his antlers held high. Lifting his head he uttered a guttural, coughing roar. The rutting went on for many nights. Mostly, by day, the herd browsed on the lush grass growing along the nearby rides and rested up on the slope beneath the oaks, while the leaves, copper, yellow and amber drifted down onto the thick carpet of last year's leaf litter. The buck was always positioned higher up the slope. He constantly patrolled around the does, keeping them in a close group and if another buck appeared, he would charge after it, blaring a challenge.

A November gale swept through the wood and the last acorns fell like stones. Buckie grew restless. Cloud shadows raced over the hillside where the herd sat, chewing their cud, their coats now a dull mud colour, ready for winter. Even the buck drowsed now, his fever subsiding. A Hogshades magpie alighted beside his tail, cocked his head and jumped on his back. The buck never moved as the magpie sauntered up the black ridge of his spine fur, stopping now and then to probe for ticks. At the buck's right ear, the bird jumped off, stalked back to the rear end and started all over again, a flash of pale sunlight striking green and blue lights from its long tail. Buckie, who was half-grown now, stood up and stretched, a tassel of fur on his small belly revealing his maleness. Wandering over to the menil fawn, he tried to butt foreheads, but the other would not play. Buckie drifted eastwards up the slope while the great buck drowsed on. The magpie had moved to a doe now and was working up her spine, against the lay of her coat. Buckie paused now and then to nibble a seedling pine or some grass in the clearings. Round the furrowed, fissured bole of a huge oak that was streaked with sea-green lichens, he was startled into a wild leap off all four legs and let out a bleat of terror at the sight of great, strange-smelling, grunting beasts. He galloped flat out back down the hill, swerving around trees to reach the safety of the herd, and even sought out his mother and huddled against her familiar flank.

Meanwhile the pigs rootled and snouted over the forest floor, churning it up until the air smelled as earthy as beetroot. They were Wessex Saddlebacks, the sows pink with enormous ears that flopped over small eyes and with a wide cummerbund of grey around each slack body. They had been let out from Marrowbones Farm to mop up the surplus acorns and prevent the Commoners' ponies from gorging themselves sick. One sow had brought her litter of ten pink, grey-belted piglets, who were romping about in the leaf litter, rolling and tumbling and squealing with excitement at this new world of freedom outside the sty. Far back in time, their ancestors, the fierce and long-snouted wild boar, had roamed these same woodlands. It took them some days to clear the acorns from the summit of Hogshades. By the time the sows had reached the does' clearing near the rutting ground, quietness lay over the wood.

The great buck, gaunt with hunger, for he had not eaten at all during the rut, hung about for a while but then moved off southwards – presently he would join up with others of his kind. Darkness gathered early under the bare oak branches and hardly ever left the deep conifer woods. The pigs gobbled up the last acorns, while a pair of jays squawked and squabbled overhead, a flash of blue wing feather the only point of colour in the winter woods. Nothing else stirred. Buckie and the does had vanished away.

3

A tree becomes a stranger

For weeks and weeks, it seemed, rain fell over the forest until the branches of pine and cedar drooped, shaggy-fronded with water like giant ferns. On Foxmoor Heath, wide sheets of water of a dull pewter colour reflected a low grey sky. Rain plopped ceaselessly into Amber Brook and bare, crimson twigs of birch dripped onto sodden ground that squelched under hoof and paw. On the great bare beeches of Kings Ash, each twig dangled a raindrop like a glass bead.

Buckie and the herd huddled for shelter under the close-planted, gloomy pines of Moonham Enclosure, moving in single file down its straight, narrow aisles to graze the rides outside when the rain eased off. When it continued all day, they stayed deep in the woods, browsing off low hanging pine branches. In the quiet of night time, water sounds thronged the air. In ditches it gurgled along, wide as streams while the oaks in Hogshades dripped dollops of water that accumulated in small hollows. The rain fell and fell, hissing softly through the pines over Buckie's head. He was restless, feeling caged by the ruled rows of trunks and the seemingly unchanging darkness. Now and then, he and the other fawns would chase each other round a pine or have a shoving match, forehead to forehead, but there was little space for fun.

One twilight, the menil fawn barged into Buckie and then ran off down a ridge between the trunks, his pale rump disappearing through the brown air. Buckie dashed after him and they collided. Next he shot past and ran on and on until he burst out into the rain onto a puddled gravel track, with the menil close behind him. Sprung as if from prison, they set off at a wild gallop, going nowhere. The two little bucks tore along neck and neck, eyes shining with glee, until a gate blocked their way. Skidding to a halt on the soft track, they snuffed at the wooden bars. Then a door slammed in the nearby cottage. Buckie leapt straight in the air, barked with fright and set off back along the path running faster and faster, his eyelashes furred with raindrops and coat slick with water, the menil close behind. At last they slowed down and dared to look round. No danger followed them so Buckie reared three times, pawing the air, brave again and bouncy. The menil trotted over and licked his left ear thoroughly, inside and out, while the rain dripped from their short tails. Sedately then, they walked back through the dark passageways of Moonham pines and rejoined the resting herd. Buckie's mother hardly noticed his return but just lifted her head, pine needles hanging from her moving jaws. She took little care of him now for another fawn grew within her. Buckie was never the same again after that spell of freedom. In the world it might still be January, but within his small body it seemed that spring had come.

February brought glimpses of pale sunlight, striping the rides with long shadows even at noon. The herd moved on at last, grazing its way down the western edge of Hogshades, returning to Amber Great Wood where the fawns had space to chase around the widespread, old trees and browse on bramble shoots which had kept their leaves all winter beneath the sheltering boughs. Buckie heard a new sound. Amber Brook had burst its banks and filled Amber Bottom with a sheet of turgid water that flung pools far into the woods on either side. Out in the middle the current roared and raced frighteningly fast, whipping along dead twigs and rafts of pale foam. Mere ditches had become tributary streams, swelling the torrent, flooding the forest floor, leaching earth from beneath a tangle of snaking roots. A hundred dead leaves and a drowned vole swept past and soon were gone. Leaning forwards, Buckie peered at unfamiliar shapes. Constantly now, he was all too evidently torn between the excitement of going off alone and the safe feeling of having the herd all about him, his mother among them. She was busy stripping dark and succulent ivy from the bole of an oak, relishing the change after weeks of pine and bramble. Here and there, grey-green clumps of foxglove leaves were pushing up through the deep leaf litter, but Buckie already knew about their dangerous, acrid taste and had learned to leave them alone.

Moss brought the only touch of colour to the woods. Little mounds of pale green bun moss thrived in all the wet places. Darker star moss grew in the wet crannies between the roots and bright green ferny stuff had crept over every long-fallen branch and trunk. Sea-green lichen crusted upon growing trees or hung from them in fuzzy tufts. Now that the showers were fewer and lighter, Amber Brook began to fall back within its banks, leaving shallow pools behind that revealed bare roots like twisted ropes and banks of shining mud, pale brown as milk chocolate. As the river's roar subsided, the wood's small sounds could be heard again – a nuthatch tapping away and jays squawking. Buckie grazed across a ride above a herd of ponies and then was brought up short by a strange smell. Other herds often met with his own, grazing along with them for a time, before wandering off again. Once, when he was quite small, a great red stag had galloped through Cuckoo Copse, bellowing for hinds, but this smell was different again.

The roe deer had sniffed out Buckie, and knew him to be harmless so they went on feeding. Ever since the twins had been born the previous May, their family had kept together. The doe was no bigger than Buckie and the buck himself was not much taller, but his short, forked antlers would be wickedly sharp later in the year. In their grey-brown winter coats the colour of wet, fallen leaves, they lived secretly in the deepest woods; not even Keeper knew of this family. Buckie stepped delicately forward towards the twins – they were smaller, might they play? But they backed away, looking round for their mother. Buckie was too big a playmate.

The waters of Amber Brook lapsed back into their proper channels with surprising speed, for a great wind blew up from the northwest. It dried the land, waking the sodden woods and at last whipped the grey, cloud blanket off the forest to reveal a sky of palest eggshell blue. The sun striped Amber Great Wood with shadows of trunk and twig while the riverbank steamed gently. The deer had lain down to chew their cud but stood again, watching small eddies of air racing by and lifting the old, brown leaves in miniature whirlwinds. Sunshine brought back the colours, flashing silver from birch boles and a glowing crimson from their drooping twigs. Across the brook, self-sown pines tossed sea-green needles and bare, knobbly larch boughs warmed to rust-red. Even the trampled, wet leaves took on coppery tints. Restless for a change, Buckie darted ahead as soon as the herd started to move on. Amber Great Wood had sheltered them well for a time, but its slope faced northwest, catching little of the low winter sun. Does and young ones trotted down to the stream, leaving neat hoof prints in the drying mud and splashing across onto the open, southerly slope of Ferny Wood. A little herd of chestnut ponies were there already; five of them stood round an oak in the sun, forelocks almost touching the trunk and backs at right angles to it, like the spokes of a wheel. Their rough winter coats made them look fatter than they really were, and with heads drooping lower and lower, they drowsed on unmoving as Buckie passed, their tails hardly stirring in the mild air.

The does had found a sunny patch, half encircled by holly thickets and gorse. One by one they came in and settled down, the bright February sunshine revealing lines of spots and their ears held at a quarter-to-three position. Only their jaws moved. There were a dozen in the herd now comprising does and young ones, yet a human eye might easily have missed them altogether on the patched brown floor of the wood.

Buckie alone wandered on. One of the hollows, which in summer provided lush grazing, was now filled with rainwater and rotting leaves, brackish, black and dead. He peered down at small hooves deep in dark mud and then he backed away. Further on, a flock of mistle thrushes fed on the remaining berries of a holly that still showed white scars where its boughs had been hacked away before Christmas. Suddenly Buckie stopped with his head tall and ears held high. A wood pigeon flew up from the top of an oak with a fussy flapping and the thrushes took to the air, wheeling across the clearing, showing pale, silvery sides of their underwings. Keeper and his labrador were coming up the track and Buckie vanished away into the shadows of a small pine grove, while they passed by. For many months he had followed his mother everywhere and had felt secure and safe surrounded by the herd. But now, in his first solitary wanderings, his senses were sharpened and he was alert to every new scent and sound in Ferny Wood.

From high up in one of the older oaks came the tap-tap of a woodpecker, prospecting the bark for grubs. No danger there. He moved on, pausing to graze untrampled grass under the curve of a fallen ash. Cattle had been round and about, big Friesians that had eaten off much of the sward, trampling heavy-bodied over the soft ground. He reached for succulent looking tuft but then jumped backwards on all four hooves, his dark eyes wide. He did not run far but nosed back towards the strange thing, inquisitively snuffing at it. It looked, at first, like a hurtling fur snake. The leading squirrel had just dug up an acorn and held it in his teeth, while his three brothers and sisters furiously chased after, snarling like small puppies. They disappeared up the nearest oak, with a scritch-scratch of claws, shaking the high twigs into commotion and disturbing the woodpecker, who flew off with his loud laughing cry, his olive-green and scarlet plumage dulled by the dimming air. Sensing another disturbance, Buckie whipped round to find the darkening spaces of the wood full of deer; the herd had moved up behind him. One of the little bucks pranced over and gave him a playful shoulder-shove before dancing away sideways. So, once more, they were all around him, protective and tall. His mother trotted over and licked his hind parts thoroughly, just as she had always done. So as dusk fell they were all once more together, moving silently up Thorny Gutter.

Morning found Buckie alone again on the edge of Amy's Lawn, peering out at a new shape that had appeared in the middle. Around it a flock of lapwings had just settled to feed; they were on their way south to case the creeks and estuaries for nesting sites. They spread out over the grass, running a few steps or flying a yard or two on their blunt, black wings, white underparts showing as they probed the soft turf for insects. As the sun rose behind the eastern curve of Hogshades, the birds lost their flat, black and whiteness and their dark backs and little crests shone blue-green as they caught the light. Out in the middle of them stood this strange apparition. Keeper had meant to light a bonfire out here, well away from any trees. The holly cutters had thrown down spiky, bare boughs, everywhere and he had collected all these into a huge pile, but had decided to wait a little longer for it to dry out, before setting it alight. So as the sun rose and the lapwings ascended in a black and white cloud, wheeling away southwards, crying 'pee-wee', that pile of green and white remained.

Buckie squeezed under the wire fence, where generations of hooves had caved a slot in the bank, his small body quick and lithe. He regarded the new object and then took a step or two towards it, snuffing forwards. Soon, he was circling the pile, watching it sideways with his big, dark eyes. When three other young deer joined him on the Lawn, he went right up to the pile and nosed it, and then jumped back. Nothing happened so Buckie leapt in the air, obviously elated with his own bravery and tore off round the heap, pursued by the others in a glorious rodeo. All the young ones took off at a gallop, racing neck-and-neck around the pile, until Buckie slowed down, bouncing on all four legs, pronking to a halt. When they set off again, some of the does who by now had caught up, joined in the fun. Buckie found he could fly right off the ground, all four hooves in the air. He reared up on his hind legs then bucked, tossing up small hooves and silently flew off again over the turf. Racing with the other fawns, arching his back, jumping high, skidding round, eyes wild, he set off on a mad circuit of Ivy's Lawn. Only in the full heat of noon did he and the rest slow down and finally subside on the grass.

That evening, the boar badger woke up from a deep satisfying sleep in his sett on the edge of Amy's Lawn and snuffed the close air of his tunnel, knowing that something was wrong. Padding up the dark tunnel, he found it blocked off from the outer air, though he could always use one of his other entrances. Next morning, Mouse Acre car park, up to the north of Malwood, sprang to life, filled with horseboxes. There were Landrovers, girls on ponies, men in red coats and a sea of eager hounds with their tails up. The blast of the horn brought some sort of order and soon all set off, following the Master in his tall black horse, heading along Buckherd Lane toward Amy's Lawn.

After the rodeo, the deer had grazed and ambled their way slowly during the night into the north-west of Ferny Wood. Buckie was feeding along a footpath that wound between crab apple, old bracken and young pine, but at the first sound of a shod hoof, his head went up and with ears forward, he trotted over to the others. The herd had been dispersed about the wood but now they began to bunch together, facing towards the alien sounds of hoof and human voices. At the first whiff of dog, they wheeled about and ran silently away among the oaks and hollies.

The dog fox and his mate from Moonham had themselves hunted through Ferny Wood that night, so their scent lay threaded everywhere, fresh enough to excite the hounds. Bursting with energy, they crashed through the wood, eyes shining, wet noses down, sniffing and snuffling, pale dogs patched with russet and black and wild for a chase. The deer had not run far and Buckie smelt the hounds coming. If they had found one strong line of scent and all followed it, the fallow deer would just have drifted to one side, but with the dogs spread throughout the wood, there was only one thing to do. They all took off at a gallop: does, yearlings, fawns as one. They sprang through the trees, black hooves skimming the leaf litter, running at full stretch. Buckie ran up at the front near his mother, keeping up well, as the last oaks and birches of Ferny Wood disappeared behind them. The hounds had found a fresh scent of a young fox and were running him down to Amber Bottom. As the noise of the hunt died away, the deer slowed, paused and tested the air with necks stretched. Then they wandered apart and slowly, some settled down to graze. But to Buckie it was all new. They were out on Furzy Common, a high, undulating stretch of moorland rising up to high, heathery hills and dipping into hollows. It was patched here and there with bracken and gorse and with seedling birch growing in a dip below the bare, rust-coloured branches of a larch plantation. At last, he settled to graze, finding new flavours in the herbage for among the coarse grasses, leaves of shepherd's sorrel and plantain had over-wintered.

The fox hunt streamed down into Amber Bottom, raced past Goathorn, spread out over Bushy Meads and lost the scent miles away on the banks of Bracken Water. Belle was an elderly spaniel, golden and tubby, being walked by her master up from the car park below but to Buckie, the merest whiff of dog meant the hunt was starting all over again. So off he ran, back to the herd. All round them stretched a brown sea of heather bushes, seemingly dead, under a vast pale sky. Calming down, he found a few half-dried-out bilberries, but when five plump brown birds whirred up right under his nose, he leapt into the air in fright, staring out over the heath long after the partridges had glided back into cover. Never again would he take the safety of his forest world for granted; all the day's alarms and chivvyings had tuned eyes, ears and nose to constant alertness.

A wild, orange light gilded the dead bracken, so that it glowed as if lit from within. The sky above remained a cold blue, but in the west the clouds had broken up and drifted, smoky-peach against fiery red. Against such brightness, every thicket and western pine stood out in black silhouette. As the sun sank, the strong colours flowed away, merged at last into greyness and the first owl cry came from Malwood. As if this were some awaited signal, the fallow deer began to move away eastwards, walking now, their brown coats matching the old heather and merging into the darkening air. They swerved south and trotted safely across the tarmac of Buckherd Lane. Then climbing a bank, they ducked under the fence at a deer-scrape and found themselves at last, in shelter hidden away under towering Douglas firs that were widespread, yet enclosing. One by one they sank down in a loose group, chewing their cud, the day's alarms fading away with last light, each body shaping a couch for itself in the deep carpet of old needles. Buckie chewed for a while then stretched out on his side.

By the time the first stars shone above the lofty, sighing branches Buckie, who usually felt most sprightly at dusk, was asleep. He was even oblivious of the male tawny owl who landed in the tree above, crying 'hoo-hoo-hoo-oo'. Presently the owl's mate landed beside him, mewing softly, then they flew away together, seeming to float in the darkness between the firs, not hunting for once, but prospecting for a nest hole. The first small stirrings of spring were visible only as one pale leaf on a honeysuckle bine.

Deep in the night, Buckie awoke and rolled onto his back. He gave one enormous stretch and with a light bound was on his feet, feeling hungry. The herd had spread across the Enclosure and through the darkness came sounds of tearing grass, the rustle of a wood mouse, and the distant cries of the owls, now hunting over Foxmoor. Buckie found the edge of a ride where the grass was quite juicy; his mother was grazing there already with the menil doe. But with the first grey light of dawn he wandered away, sniffing and peering at emerging shapes along the southern border. The first leaves of violets provided a new flavour and he ate all those he could find on the bank. Further on, he stopped to investigate a dark shape as nearly as tall as himself, looming above the line of the bank. As it stayed still and only smelled earthy, he ventured closer. The wood ants had built a castle several feet high and thick-thatched with fir needles. Huddled together close about their queen, they slept deep beneath it and would not stir until the sun warmed their roof and drew them upwards. It provided nothing to eat, so Buckie wandered back into the wood. Just inside, heaps of newly-turned stones shone sandy-gold in the dim air, for the boar badger had needed to dig out all the entrances that had been blocked up for the foxhunt. He was just padding up one of his familiar paths through Moonham after a satisfactory night eating rabbit, but down below in the nursery chamber, where he was not allowed to go, the sow lay fast asleep. Two blind cubs, born on the previous day, cuddled against her, their bare little bellies replete with milk and their pale grey foreheads showing just a ghost of the darker stripes to come. Now and then they twitched and pushed closer into their mother's furry warmth.

Buckie moved on, as restless as ever, a light easterly breeze blowing from behind him. Buckie still had a lot to learn. High above, the firs sighed together and all around him stood their great trunks, row upon row; only a few scrubby elder had managed to push up between them in the dim air. Suddenly, one of the shorter pillars moved. Buckie reared in fright and shock and then once more galloped away at full stretch down the long aisles between the Douglas firs, until he glimpsed a placidly grazing doe and slowed down. He was back among the herd – and safe.

Meanwhile, the stranger had slouched away.

4

Yearling

Pale flowers were the first to glimmer into sight in the cool April dawn: primroses, growing everywhere in the rank grass and across Ivy's Lawn and delicate panicles of wild cherry, just breaking open their hanging heads, still beaded with the night's rain. A blackbird whistled up the sun and two great tits sang 'preacher-preacher' in competition, while a thrush tried his melodious phrase, over and over. A woodpecker, on his way to the ants' castle, added a flash of olive green as he looped past. With the waking day, the fallow deer left the Lawn where they had grazed all night and ambled back, one by one, into the dark shelter of Moonham, using a well-trampled scrape in the bank where they could duck under the wire. The bumps on Buckie's forehead were just beginning to sprout horns, showing the first small V shape of a pricket. He sat and chewed the cud for an hour in the permanent twilight beneath the dark green, whispering canopy, with eyes half closed and ears slack. The rest of the herd surrounded him, dozing, ruminating and quiet. Their security folded about him like a blanket for what was to be the last time. Nearly as tall as his mother now, he stood up and stretched his back legs, waiting. None of the others moved so he trotted away by himself down one of the straight aisles, his black, ridged tail whisking over his white rump until he came to a long bank where violets grew. The bank broke up the geometric lines of trees, letting in some dappled sunlight. Here he paused to graze on the violets of Moonham Castle.

Long ago, even before the Romans came to the forest and built their kilns beyond Malwood, men had raised these banks to house their women, children or cattle against some tribal raid, overseas invader or wolves. The low, broken mounds would never tell their secrets. Buckie wandered through a gap which may have been the main entrance – or a mistake by a Forestry tractor. There never was a less pretentious castle than Moonham, though beloved of pearl-bordered fritillaries who flittered through the pines in a brightness of amber, to lay their eggs on whatever violet plants Buckie had left. He moved on now to sample fresh birch buds at the wood's edge, until he was disturbed by a crashing of twigs made by a buck that cantered out onto the track, wild-eyed. He had just lost his left antler and blood still seeped from the broken socket. The remaining antler was a fine specimen, three-tined and broadly palmated, but now it was just a useless weight on his right side. Finding a gap in Moonham pines he jumped the fence in one tight, graceful curve and was instantly wrapped about by their darkness. Buckie peered at this new sight and set to follow.

Ducking under the fence, he scraped off a last tuft of old brown coat. A female chaffinch, building her moss-cup nest in a thorn bush nearby, teased out some of the wiry hairs and flew back to line her nest. Seven journeys she made in all, the pale April sun lighting her subtle fawns and greys, while the cock bird, bright in his chestnut, black, white and slate blue, pecked about feeding himself among a flock of tits. Buckie lost track of the one-antlered buck and wandered back toward the ruined cottage. The twisted old trees, planted when the cottage was built, still strove to put forth leaves here and there and even a pink button of bud. He nosed the long, wet grass but it was far too late for apples. There was a tap-tap from overhead – a nuthatch was enlarging a hole in the Bramley apple tree for a nest site. He peered at the bank where a female adder had slithered out to absorb what warmth she could from the thin spring rays of sun. She lay in a loose hank of sepia scales zig-zagged with black, relaxed it seemed, even asleep, but a tiny gold eye stayed wide open. Buckie avoided her. A single peacock butterfly that had over-wintered in the old pony shed flew down to sample a primrose, then a dandelion, since the late spring offered so little to eat.

Keeper had been doing his hated paperwork most of the day. Evening was time for a stretch in the fresh air; he might go up and see if the young badgers were out. Why not, he deserved a treat after all those forms! Thin grey cloud covered the sky now and twilight would fall early. Already, across Ivy's Lawn, the cherry blossom shone pale against the darkness of Cuckoo Copse. He licked a finger and held it up. What breeze there was blew from the west, he would have to approach from the east then so as not to bolt the badgers back into their sett.

So he eased his bulk under the fence into Moonham Wood taking care not to disturb the young buck that he could see out on the copse edge. The poachers had never materialised, they would probably wait for early autumn which was their favourite time. His plan was still in order though, the Police being ready to immobilise any van they found nearby, as soon as he gave them the tip-off. Suddenly, the little buck's head jerked up – had Keeper cracked a twig? No, the deer was looking away from him in the darkening air. Sweeping his glasses in an arc, he glimpsed a human shape. The person was clever, remaining still – and soon the buck had gone back to grazing. Of course, the person could just be another innocent deer-watcher since dusk was always a good time to catch them out in the open. Keeper turned quietly homeward without revealing his presence, moving softly from tree to tree through the darkening pines. "Best get back to the phone, just in case" he thought. His contact would not have his mobile number.

It rang as soon as he reached home.

"Tonight," a female voice whispered, "Cuckoo Copse," and rang off. He called the Police, warning them that it could be a false alarm, but they agreed to take no chances. Then he set out, armed with his largest flashlight, in the Landrover. He would drive part of the way. The poachers would have lights too, of course, to dazzle the deer and make them look up. They would also have fast dogs, lurchers. Leaving the vehicle a quarter of a mile away from the spot, he set off at a clumsy run. They weren't having that beautiful young buck. Soon he slowed down. They would surely wait until it was quite dark. Maybe that had been an advance scout that he had glimpsed.

On the edge of Cuckoo Copse, Buckie, oblivious to danger, was grazing with relish on the new little flowers that were just beginning to push up their leaves: dandelions, chickweed, cats ear and clover. All seemed quiet and still; even the little owl had flown away, silent as a shadow. He had wandered further out onto the Lawn in the dark when suddenly, a great light flashed out and there was the sound of a shot and shouts and great dogs racing about. Keeper's light caught the armed poacher right in the eyes, even as he aimed at Buckie, so the shot went wild.

Buckie was off, galloping for his very life. Keeper gave the Police ten minutes before calling them up. Yes, they had picked up four poachers trying to start their van and they could be properly charged with poaching as they had been seen to shoot. Sometimes it was not so easy, as although you could catch a gang with dogs and guns they would swear that they were only bird watching!

Far out over Foxmoor, dawn silvered the still surface of the pool and a large, greyish bird awoke, stretched his long black neck and slid off the island for the first weed-dabble of the day. Buckie watched the Canada goose upend, its pale rump pointing to the brightening sky. The night's commotion had broken the last ties with his mother and the herd. He galloped away from the terrible bang and lights and reek of dog and had slowed down when all was quiet again, but had then gone trotting on through the wiry bushes of Foxmoor, just as the herd had done that other time. Now he grazed on some succulent grass by the pool's edge before moving back into gorse cover. Finding a cave-like space under the thick branches that just fitted him, he settled down to chew the cud, and even drowsed off to sleep. Some tiny, pale feathers were caught in the spines above his head.

Meanwhile, the pond world was waking up. Like many other pools in the Forest it was man-made, a flooded gravel pit. On its final run, the bulldozer had piled up two big mounds of gravel out in the middle and even as it roared away, the forest had begun to take over, seeding the banks and islands. Now heather, small green snouts of bracken, and gorse thickets spread right down to the bank on two sides, while old woods sheltered the pool to the west and north. The islands, untrodden by humans, had sprouted thickets of birch scrub, fringed with willow that dipped their branches right down into the greenish water. Willow and birch were spun with pale green buds against a background of dark needles of Scots pine, which sighed in a chill breeze from the west. The goslings slept warmly though in a soft, down-lined nest under a drooping willow, covered by the thick feathers of their mother until she, too, awoke and sailed out onto the water without a splash, handsome in her black and white plumage.

A vast, cold blue sky arched over the heath as the early sunshine lay calm and very quiet over the pool, all fresh and serene. The gander swam round the smaller island to meet his mate, leaving only the faintest ripple behind. For a while, they dabbled for weed together, then she returned to the nest and swam back again, this time followed by the three goslings. They were gawky in their baby feathers and paddled frantically to keep up, their small necks stretched with effort. They landed on the bank close to Buckie, picked about and flapped wings so short that it seemed impossible that they would ever fly. The gander came up out of the water and marched round, his big black webbed feet slapping the gravel, on guard. The goose had actually hatched four eggs, but she had stayed out too late the previous night – a vixen had slid out of the gorse thicket, snatched a gosling and vanished into the shadows. Since it was not large enough to feed her cubs back in their den under a hollow oak, she had sat down under the same gorse bush where Buckie now drowsed and gobbled up the morsel.

A crunching of gravel, followed by a loud bang woke Buckie and in a second he was on his feet and running away, quick and silent. The people reached into their car for folding chairs, slamming doors and calling out to each other, but they never so much as glimpsed a deer's tail. A moorhen had also shot under the cover of the willows, churning the water. But the brown mallard mother who nested among the reeds against the smaller island came swimming boldly out in search of crumbs, closely followed by nine yellow ducklings who followed her every movement, as if on leads. More cars and picnickers arrived so Buckie moved further off, but finding less cover out on the bare, heathery stretches of Foxmoor, he made for the northern woods travelling in a wide half circle. By evening, as the last car drove away, he had returned to the pond, drawn by the lush grass at the water's edge. As he grazed in the dusk with all the light draining westwards, the water dulled to a pewter gleam and a nuthatch landed fearlessly by his muzzle. It scooped up a beakful of mud and then flashed off to the nearest oak tree. All day the bird had flown to and fro, like a dart of amber and slate-blue, plastering the entrance hole of her nest chamber. The entrance was too wide and would have allowed a hungry squirrel access to raid. A single swallow skimmed the pool, sweeping up a sip of water on the wing. Soon only pale colours shone through the twilight, made by the swallow's breast, the gander's cheek patch, a scatter of lady's smock on the bank, Buckie's rump and a motionless, vertical streak by the smaller island. Presently, this 'streak' plunged a long beak into the water and then the heron, its grey body soon lost in the grey air, flew off with his trout.

Buckie stayed for a time on Foxmoor, learning to hide up in the thickets by day and returning to the pool for a quiet's night grazing, but soon there were more cars staying for longer periods so he moved right away into the northern woods. Slowly, a late, cold spring was raising sap in growing plants; honeysuckle bines had been out for weeks, pale against the dark trunks to which they clung. As he wandered through King's Ash, new silvery beech buds burst, shedding their papery scales. On the edge of Skythorns Ridge, dark stems were scattered with white flowers delicate as snowflakes. "Ah, blackthorn winter", the locals said. Buckie gnawed the bark of a young sycamore and found it sweet with sap.

He wandered west seeking more and hence came to the brink of Ocknell Bottom.

Here the heath plunged down into a great green bowl surrounded by rising woods on the far side. From the brink their canopy spread below like a vast patterned quilt, the green of new beech brilliant against patches of dark fir. Tassels of larch were a richer green beside the amber tassels of oak, with ash in sooty flower and birch quivering in showers of green over silver. Buckie trotted down the steep slope. Once at the bottom, he found juicy grass everywhere and encircling woods for cover. It was like Ivy's Lawn but on a larger scale. Plantain, sorrel and chickweed grew here too and the oaks hung out their yellow catkin clusters. Under a pine at the forest's edge, a strange communal urge moved among the wood ants, with the coming of the dry, mild airs of May. For years, their castle of pine needles had stood there, three feet high, thatched against winter storms, constantly extended and repaired. But now, they had decided to build a new one, six feet to the west. Buckie peered at the dark ribbon of ants along the bank dragging fragments of dry needles to the new nest site, or returning for more. He left it alone. As days passed, the first tiny pile grew primrose-high as white violets came into bloom and wood sorrel hung out fragile white flowers among its shamrock leaves. Buckie stayed in Ocknell Bottom, losing the remainder of his dull, old coat, until he was immaculate in glowing chestnut, dappled with white while the bumps on his forehead elongated at last into two sprigs of horn. Three mares and their foals often grazed with him. By day he would browse through the woods, chewing sweet new leaves of birch and beech where they hung low enough. Where oaks stood widespread, bluebells covered the ground in a sky-blue haze and high above, the canopy trembled all day with bird song and flitting wings. In this calm, he put on weight and although he sometimes met small herds of fallow does, he stayed alone.

One evening, when hawthorn flowers on the hillside glimmered pale through the twilight, scenting the still air, Buckie was grazing out in the centre of this great bowl. A thrush still sang deep in the woods, repeating his little tunes over and over as gnats danced in small compact clouds and the ants worked steadily on, moving house. Out of the dusk came a sudden rustling, then a cracking of twigs and a herd of red deer, big stags in shining, rufous coats and growing antlers, broke from the trees and cantered out onto the grass. They slowed down and stood together, heads held high, looking around, before one by one moving a few steps apart and beginning to graze. Buckie had sprung for cover at the first crack of a twig, although only to just inside the wood. As quiet flowed back and moths flickered out, he moved soundlessly between the great trunks and peered out from behind an oak, snuffing the air, curious as ever. The large, slow bodies seemed no real threat. After watching for a time, he stole along, keeping just inside the woodland edge, one neat hoof destroying three weeks' work by the wood ants on their new castle. Finally, he came out to graze again on the grass furthest away from the big deer.

They stayed, taking no notice of Buckie, yet he constantly raised his head, looking over towards their dark bulk, feeling unsettled and vaguely threatened. When a half-moon came up over Foxmoor, he stood for a moment, quite still except for his moving jaws, then he turned and set off southwards. He climbed up out of the great hollow, crossing miles of heather west of the pond, until he came to a cottage that smelled of man and dog. Night hung deeply over the forest now. The tarmac gleamed in the moonlight but all seemed quiet, so he trotted across and found the Common rising up ahead. Up he climbed between gorse thickets, heather bushes and sandy hollows, following deer paths and rabbit tracks. The first light of a June morning found him on the summit of Furzy Common, a high, undulating spread of moorland patched with bright green bracken half-uncurled, with a vast view into far blue distances of unknown counties. He browsed on new sprigs of heather, tormentil and shepherd's sorrel growing round the edge of a bare, sandy hollow. Below, a herd of black and white cattle from Jack's farm crossed the road and ambled up onto the Common as they did every morning of their lives, but he took no notice. It was something much smaller which made him start upright and jump two steps back.

Sunshine, golden and warm, lay on the Common, soaking into the earth, drawing an elusive scent from all the sun-coloured gorse flowers: an essence of summer. The female adder had crawled slowly out of her chilled night-hole, still lethargic and dull with cold, into the sandy hollow and slowly arranged her length in a loose hank on the northwest slope. She lay as still as stone, apparently asleep, although the tiny eye never closed. She was a young snake, her underscales still with a coppery shine beneath the dark chocolate zig-zags down her back. It was the male adder, whipping fast and keen through the heather, which had disturbed Buckie. He slithered down into the hollow, sun-warmed and eager as the female raised her head. His neck rubbed gently against hers.

Buckie watched as they delicately twined and wreathed about each other in a courtship ritual as old as the hill beneath them. The male was older, larger, and handsomely marked with bold black down his long shining body that was the colour of old oak leaves.

A drumming of hooves made Buckie retreat into the gorse. The Saturday morning pony club horses and riders shook the ground with their drumming hooves and shouts of glee. The hill at once became alive with red and blue anoraks, shining helmets, flying tails, excited shouts – but all were gone in a moment. As silence returned, a small bird flew up from Buckie's bush and perched on its topmost branch, appearing black against the light, but the true colours were subtler shades of slate, brown and chestnut. The Dartford Warbler opened his beak, 'churr-churred' for a moment and then flew away to search for spiders while below him, deep in the bush, his mate incubated three eggs in a neatly-woven nest of stems lined with black and white cattle hair. All day larks sang, spiralling urgently up and down in the blue air.

At twilight, Buckie wandered on across the Common heading southwards until, on its steep slope, he was brought up short by a tall fence. Enticing pale green leaves of birch poked through the wire mesh. He nibbled them and tried to pull more branches through the holes. The deer fence seemed to protect a plantation of birches no more than five feet high, their leaves shimmering and trembling in the darkening air. In fact, the Forestry Commission had planted and fenced twelve acres of Scots pine, one of their regular, quick-growing cash crops. Unchecked by grazing, little seedling birches had sprung up everywhere and were being allowed to grow on for a time as nurse trees to the infant conifers. Buckie trotted along the whole length of the fence, knowing it was too high to leap. Soon it turned at a right angle and continued on, hard and unchewable, but others had been there before him. Near the corner, rabbits had burrowed right down under the buried wire, softening the bank. Other deer had scraped at it with their pointed hooves and finally, one had squeezed under, deepening the scrape, so Buckie only had to duck through and there he was among all the sweetness. He stayed for some days, gorging on juicy, delicious leaves while the first foxglove bells opened at the wood's edge, while above, on the Common, the Dartford Warblers flew frantically to and fro with beakfuls of spiders for their three nestlings.

On Midsummer's Day he scrambled out of the Enclosure, restless again and ambled downhill, pausing to graze now and then until he came back to Ferny

Wood. It was a sultry summer's evening, the trees hanging their branches heavy and still while thunder rolled around the horizon. A distant cuckoo was calling 'cuck-cuck' with its broken voice and only bees were still moving in the warm air. All day they had followed a flight path from their nest in the old cherry tree to some tall spires of foxglove. As the last of them flew home and a tawny owl's long, hollow cry floated out over Malwood, Buckie passed the hidden nest where he had been born. Today, all unknowingly, he had become a yearling. His coat glowed in the dusk, a thin black line running down his back and tail and round the white heart-shaped rump patch. The V-shaped horns were finger long and still growing. The months alone had made him alert and strong. Deeper in that same wood, his mother grazed near her week-old fawn – but Buckie would never recognise her again.

As the first stars shone out, he found some lush grass sheltered by the bulk of a fallen oak. The dog fox from Cuckoo Copse slunk by, heading for the rabbit bank and a small bat flittered overhead, gnat hunting. A slight rustle amid a stand of pines made Buckie look up, tall-necked, ears high, ready to pronk away but as he smelled only his own kind he relaxed and lowered his head again to the grass. The fallow deer which stole out from the shadowy pines and came to graze beside him was a year older, a sorrel, with small, one-branched antlers. All night they grazed or slept, side by side, and when dawn came and Buckie moved off to chew his cud, the sorrel came too and lay down on the needles close by. All summer they stayed together, often grazing many yards apart but always returning to chew their cud, side by side. Sometimes they played round the fallen oak in the long summer evenings, flying through the air, gleeful and mad.

One evening, while the redstarts flew to and fro with the last of the day's feed for their nestlings on the old shed, a single adult buck came galloping by, streamers of tattered velvet flying from his antlers. He was in a wild hurry although nothing pursued him. Buckie followed him at a trot with the sorrel following, but soon the buck was outsight. They wandered into the sheltering Moonham for a few days and then ambled back to Ivy's Lawn. The leaves on the wild cherry were turning crimson now and a squirrel sat on the gatepost, bathed in the sun's last rays. The woodpecker looped past, a mere flash of green, paying his last visit of the day to the wood ant's castle. A herd of does grazed in the overgrown orchard, raiding the twisted old trees after dark. Little had changed there – only Buckie himself.

For a few days, he and the sorrel grazed about the fringes of Ivy's Lawn and

Cuckoo Copse. Bucks often passed by now, seemingly always on urgent business. As the first crimson cherry leaves fell, a new restlessness invaded Buckie, an excitement in his loins he had never felt before. When twilight invaded the woods and the little owl flew to his perch above the rowan's brilliant berries, Buckie and his companion stole out of the copse and then set off eastwards side by side, their small antlers high and proud.

A great time was about to begin.

5

The secret paths of night

The sun rose on a colourless, glimmering world, heathland grey with heavy night dews, every grass blade weighed down with drops of water that blurred the green and the great stretch of Foxmoor lost beneath a still, white mist. Not so much as a birch leaf trembled. Buckie and the sorrel made the only small movements as they grazed slowly along a runnel flowing in the pool that seeped out of its narrow, peaty banks to form a patch of bog that the young deer grazed with relish.

Deep in the spongy sphagnum moss grew sundews, their flowers dead now, but still holding up red-fringed leaves to lure a passing fly to its death. Bog asphodel was over for the season too, but its orange seed pods stood bright as flowers among a few tattered flags of cotton grass. A sprig of bog myrtle, crushed by Buckie's hoof, wafted a strong fragrance around him with a warm tang, like mingled balsam and pine. By the time he reached the pool the mist was drifting away upwards, still hiding the branches of the tall oak and beech in Kings Ash Enclosure, but now their massive boles were revealed. Below the trees, just inside the fence, half a dozen fallow buck were lying down and chewing their cud, their broad antlers bone-smooth. This was a mere remnant of what the herd had once been and soon, some of these would break away and wander off alone.

As Buckie grazed along its edge, the pool lay still and bright as a mirror, until a mallard rounded the island with three smaller ducks following behind in a line. These were this year's hatchlings, three-quarters grown now and dull-brown as yet but bright-eyed, each sending a V-shaped ripple across the shining water which stirred rafts of lily leaves, their white buds waiting for the sun.

Presently, three ponies came down the opposite bank to drink, a chestnut mare with her half-grown foal and a bay mare, barren that year, a kind of aunt to the foal. Once, they lifted dripping chins and pricked their ears at distant sounds – slamming, rattling and shouts. Too far way for danger, it seemed, so they drank again, shaking out their manes, for the flies were waking.

Now that the mist had vanished away, the sun lay warm and golden over Foxmoor in the still, September morning. Summer lingered on in wide carpets of purple heather, swallows still skimming the pool to drink although they had begun flocking together, strung along the top of the wire by Kings Ash. On the island, a single young horse chestnut tree struck a note for autumn, flaring yellow against the dark, seedling pines. As the ponies moved away to graze, a moorhen stole out of the reeds and pecked about in the quietness as pigeons called to each other in the high beeches, 'croo-croo-croo-CROO-croo', over and over. Buckie had grazed his fill and stood for a moment, the sun gilding his chestnut coat although it was not as bright as that of the big bucks in the wood. He turned his head to look at his companion, ears relaxed, peaceful. The sorrel went on grazing so Buckie ambled over to one of his resting places, where a gorse thicket made a sheltering half-moon fringed with harebells and late, tarnished sprigs of bell heather. He sat down to chew his cud in this sheltered hollow, lifted a hind hoof to scratch a tick from his ear – and shot to his feet. For the heath had suddenly burst into life, the ground shaking with the drumming of hooves and the still air torn by wild shouting, hallooing and waving. Five riders appeared, strung out across western Foxmoor, driving a straggle of ponies. Before they reached the pond, Buckie had crept deep into the gorse thicket, watching as they gathered up the two mares and the foal. The wild ponies neighed with fright, rolled their eyes and tried madly to break away at the side, but there was always a horse and rider, quick to turn them back. Larks and pipits flew up into safer air and the fallow buck vanished silently away into the deeper fastness of Kings Ash.

When Buckie and the sorrel had left Cuckoo Copse a few days before, they had met up with the buck herd on the heath and had tagged along behind and around it, wary of those great spiked and flattened antlers at their fullest spread. Now, when all seemed quiet again except for the humming of bees working the last of the heather, Buckie stole out of the thicket, ears high and forward, peering out. Both the sorrel and the buck herd had disappeared. Though there was cover of a kind out here, with small stands of birch and pine and fading bracken tall enough to hide in, compared to the woods it felt exposed with no sense of security. He hesitated, nose to the south, but once more the ground began to shake beneath his hooves; the riders were making a second sweep.

Where the steep flank of Skythornes Ridge swept down almost to the fence of Kings Ash Enclosure, making a bottleneck, there stood a permanent, rough-hewn pound. Here, the Keeper from Marrowbones Lodge clipped tails in precise patterns. Some of the mares were let out and sent off back again with much waving of caps, whooping and high whinnies, the hubbub drifting out over Foxmoor where adders basked on regardless in the noonday sun.

All the activity had made Buckie restless to leave, but he waited until the round-up was well and truly over and even the smallest heather clump was throwing a long shadow eastwards, before stealing out and beginning to move southwards at a steady trot, the sun's last rays gilding his antlers. By the time he reached Malwood, dusk had fallen beneath the soaring Douglas firs and even the wood ants were resting. A chill night wind moved among the long, hanging tresses of the firs, sighing with a murmuring swish like a distant sea. Nothing else moved until the boar badger, on watch in the mouth of his sett, a pale stripe in the darkness, padded out a few yards to squat over his latrine pit.

Buckie stayed several days in Malwood, grazing along its rides and leaping the deep, sheer-sided drainage ditches, but it was dark and solitary and not what he really wanted. Another dawn saw him moving on southwards through the edge of Cuckoo Copse. Lifting his shiny black nose, he snuffed the air and, smelling deer, he trotted out onto Ivy's Lawn where a fallow doe grazed with her fawn. When Buckie lowered his head to graze close by, they took no notice at first. When the fawn wandered over to a particularly lush clump of grass nourished by pony droppings, Buckie went too and jostled the fawn away, starting on the grass himself. The fawn stared at him with big dark eyes, then took a few steps forward to graze again but Buckie was there first, shouldering him aside. The third time this happened, the fawn skipped back to his mother and nuzzled under her, hoping for a comforting suck. It was late in the season for this but he was late-born and still small. Buckie had only wanted to play.

A robin woke in the cherry tree and began to sing, wistful and high, a red breast showing among the red leaves. Buckie ducked under the sagging wire of the fence and ambled through the wet tussocks of the abandoned orchard. The fallen apples had long since been hollowed-out by wasps. A wood mouse crept across the gatepost, black eyes bulging and whiskers whiffling while the first hornet of the day zoomed out of the old wood pile. On the edge of the wood, Buckie found a few ripe fruit on the crab apple, while magpies awoke and flew down from Malwood, squabbling over acorns at the edge of Ferny Wood and scolding each other with cries as harsh as rattles. The wood mouse took cover in a clump of ivy. Having eaten all the apples he could reach, Buckie prepared to rear up on his hind legs and reach for the higher ones. By the time he had finished, the sun had risen warmly enough to draw wisps of vapour from the gateposts and wake the first butterflies. They came to the old garden for the last few purple, side flowers on the sprawling old buddleia, although most had already turned brown and dry. Soon there were red admirals, two peacocks that looked black with their wings closed and a sprinkle of meadow browns, all flitting delicately through the flowers. A hornet, fiercely orange and yellow, flew to the top of the bush, waited, hovered, then dived and snatched a large white, nipping off its wings and flying away with the body. Buckie watched the wings drift slowly down.

The doe and fawn had moved away into Ferny Wood and joined up with four other deer. He followed them through the high, tattered bracken, turned variously yellow, brown or fox-coloured. The old grey squirrel from the pine tree drey was busy stripping nuts from the nearest hazel tree, swinging through the branches with such urgency to cause the first yellow leaves to patter down round Buckie's hooves. As yet, the holly berries were only a dull orange, although those on the rowan that the birds had left glowed a brilliant vermilion.

One grey and misty morning, when it seemed that the sun would never break through the thin cloud, Buckie and the does were grazing round a fallen oak tree, long ago girdled by squirrels. Then a truck roared down the ride nearby, stopping at the field gate with a crunch of gravel and a jingle of keys. Buckie stole away from the alien sounds and smells into a clump of ten-foot high seedling pines but he was still curious and watched the men jump down, unloading strange shapes. He did jump back at the first high, angry whining sound, but soon peered out again. Then a young pine fell across the track, disturbing two great tits and a wood mouse. Later, a nuthatch flew into a space of air where there should have been a tree. Keeper and Shadow passed by.

"Seen some queer things in these woods," said one of the Forestry workers, "but I never reckoned to be felling trees for butterflies!"

"Mm, funny old caper, but I do like to see them about," Keeper said. "The old place can do with a bit more sunshine."

Doe looking for a secluded place to give birth

A young three-month old buck and his mother

A four-day old buck, hiding in a nettle bed

Common fallow prickets, re-growing their antlers

Young tree leaves make ideal food for growing bucks

A master buck in autumn, proudly displaying his palmated antlers

A herd of common fallow bucks, aged 2-3 years

A young white buck, its ginger coat indicative of its infancy

Two menil bucks aged 2-3 and 3-4 years,
determined from their antlers

Fallow in all their colours – common, menil, black and white

There is only one way to become master buck

A herd of older bucks in late summer

A well-grown common buck, holding his antlers high

A two and a half year old buck in autumn

Winter makes it harder for the deer to forage

A group of menil deer

The master buck in autumn, heading for the rut

A white master buck with stained brush and flanks in the rut

Buckie stared out at the feast of needles suddenly made available at ground level, but he went no nearer, even after the men had driven off deeper into the woods. After all, there was plenty of juicier, softer grazing about at the moment. A cloud of plump, pale little birds passed by. These were warblers, fattening themselves up for their long journey south – the swallows were already gone.

That night, a big buck stalked into Ferny. Buckie smelled him first and then saw the tall antlers gleaming in the starlight. Every doe stopped grazing and stared, one with grass still hanging from her mouth. Even the younger ones stood still as rocks for a moment. The buck tossed his head, gave a guttural cough and trotted past to a stand of seedling pines, then lowering his splendid antlers, began to thrash them to and fro until their thin trunks began to show white scars, twigs and needles flying widely about. The still air grew heavy with his goatish smell. Soon the does returned to their grazing. When the thrashing was over, the buck stood still for a time as if listening for something and then trotted away southwards towards Amber Bottom. By morning, all the does and fawns were gone from Ferny Wood. Buckie caught up with the big buck where he was grazing lush grass beside Amber Brook and stayed with him although always a few yards behind, ranging restlessly up through Amber Great Wood and out across Blackslade. Other bucks crossed their path, thick-necked, pungent-smelling and hostile-eyed, all urgently wanting to get away from each other and find good doe country.

One still, autumn evening, when the weather still held fair, Buckie turned aside into a stand of seedling birch, their pale trunks glimmering in the dusk, although they were only a few feet high. There, Buckie began to thrash his small V-shaped antlers through the twigs, to and fro, until they were leafless. With the coming of October, the acorns lost their apple-green colour and grew brown and ripened, dropping with loud splats to the woodland floor for pigs from the farm to guzzle them up. Buckie was used to the pigs by now, although he always skirted around them. The old squirrel in Ferny Wood swung through his oak, shaking down more acorns, running down the knotted trunk so fast that he was a mere streak of grey. He buried one acorn, snatched up another and then saw a rival squirrel with a better find – a whole prickly burr of sweet chestnut. He dropped the acorn and raced after him, straight up a tall sycamore trunk. As the two ran helter-skelter through the branches, leaves as large as hands drifted down in their brilliant yellows and greens with bright pink stems.

Under the tree, Buckie and another pricket feasted on the leaves. When an especially large one spiralled down, they both reached for it and started chewing from opposite sides. When their noses touched, each stopped for a moment and they eyed each other very closely. When the leaf tore into halves, Buckie finished his portion and trotted away as if obeying some urgent signal. As darkness fell, the wood seemed alive with sounds: a distant, hard, guttural coughing; small, nervous bleatings; many hooves moving through new leaf litter; an abrupt high screaming. A great hunter's moon rose above Hogshades, yellow as an old cheese, its light filtering down onto Ferny. It striped the ground black and white, catching a flick of black tail and white rump, throwing a black gate shadow onto white grass and gleaming silver on a polished antler. It illuminated a white doe. She stood there, still as some ghostly forest presence in the centre of a glade between a crab apple and pine, until Buckie trotted up beside her. Then she also moved away through the moon shadows, a sandy fawn materialising beside her and soon all three were splashing across Amber Brook.

Morning light revealed the muddy banks on either side of the ford deeply cloven by small hooves, all prints heading southwards up the grass ride between Amber Great Wood and a plantation of young trees. Then they veered left under huge old oaks and beeches, soon to be lost in a trampled floor of churned mud that stretched away for many yards between the massive trunks, its boundaries marked by torn branches and pale, scarred boles. Buckie stood by a frayed elder sapling, excited by the rank smell and dipping his head now and then he snuffed at the edge of the black rutting floor. Groups of does wandered about the far, sunny glades of the wood, the leaves overhead glowing gold and flame and yellow and russet, against a cold, blue sky.

A robin sang out from the nearest oak, the sound as clear and sweet as a chime of tiny bells, while away up the hill came a guttural, intermittent grunting cough. The white doe, grazing near to Buckie, raised her head to listen from time to time although her jaws went on working. Presently two bucks appeared halfway up the slope, walking along side by side. One was an old buck, his antlers magnificently spread with wide palmations and many tines and beside him a younger one, about four years old, also with a good set held high and proud. However, beside those of the older buck, they seemed puny and narrow. Still together, these two came out onto a grass ride and turned downhill almost to the stream, before moving sharply off into the plantation, soon out of sight among the close-planted saplings.

All of a sudden, the wood was rent by loud clashings of antlers. Buckie peered between the shuddering trees, while a squirrel close by froze with an acorn halfway to his mouth. All up the long wooded slope, does paused in their grazing and pricked their ears. Clash–clash: like branches clattering together, like splintering bone, broken by deep grunts and loud, heavy breathing. Leaves flew from small beeches. Then, as suddenly as it had begun, the fighting stopped. A wild crashing died away on the far side of the plantation. The old buck emerged slowly, grunted, then stalked across to the centre of the rutting floor before urinating copiously.

Buckie watched, excited by the acrid smell, while the buck pranced off up the slope and approached the nearest doe, sniffing her tail. She ran coyly away, although only for a few yards. Instead of pursuing her, he sniffed along the ground behind, grunting and tossing his antlers from side to side. Another doe, and then another treated him in the same way, not yet quite in the mood. But by evening, little parties of does teetered about on the edge of the glade, looking at each other as if considering, before setting off for the rutting floor. Just as the moon arose in the eastern sky a loud, groaning cough arose from Amber Bottom and the does stared downhill, motionless, until one moved down the slope, followed by two more. The old buck was off then, galloping round to head them off, but the groaning rose up loud on the night air and more does broke away. Buckie followed them. There was no battle this time. The old buck bullied and chivvied 'his' does back up the hill, making small charges if they did not move fast enough. One ran from him with gentle bleating, but there did not seem to be many making the attempt. Buckie returned and stayed near the white doe, roused by all the activity.

For several nights, the moon-striped woods echoed with belching grunts, clashing antlers and the beating of urgent hooves, while the tawny owls called to each other from high branches and many eyes glowed yellowish-green through the darkness before vanishing away. Buckie was not mature enough to mate this year, although a few prickets born earlier in the season were ready. Even so, they were unlikely to get a chance. As yet, Buckie showed no sign of the mature buck's bodily changes; no proper thickening of the neck or opening of the glands beneath the eye and his small, male tassel still hung down instead of being flattened back against the belly. But still, an excitement stirred within him, something new and strange.

One evening, he was grazing near a huge, fallen oak where a wide gap in the canopy let in enough sunshine for grass to grow in a rough circle around the stump. Forestry men had long ago tidied up the dead branches into a heap placed several yards away. The stump sprouted shining brown fungi between cushions of moss. A sorrel deer, a year older than Buckie, grazed nearby and a squirrel sat upright on the fallen trunk, turning finicky beechmast in her long claws as she stripped off the husks. In the spring, a wren had raised nine chicks in a ball of nest wedged in a cleft of the old stump but now, a wood mouse had taken it over for the winter. The squirrel finished her nut, grabbed up another and decided to bury it. Running across the clearing with it held high in her mouth, she saw a handy hole in the stump and reached a paw towards it, just as the wood mouse shot out with black eyes shining. Taken by surprise, the squirrel let out a loud 'kiss-kiss' of alarm, startling the sorrel into dancing sideways, shouldering Buckie in the process. For a moment the two young bucks stared at each other, very close together and then Buckie shouldered back. In an instant, they were chasing each other round and round the stump, hooves flying through the darkening air, while the squirrel leapt up the nearest beech and the wood mouse shot back to its nest. Buckie jumped into the air off all his four feet and would have gone on playing, but the sorrel's heart was not in it. When a belching groan sounded from the rutting floor below, he came to a sudden stop, ears held high and forward. Then he set off downhill through the great trees with Buckie following.

All over Amber Great Wood, narrow tracks, deeply hoof-printed, led to the rutting floor where the old master paraded up and down, groaning without pause. His head was thrown back so far that the antlers touched his neck although sometimes he lowered his muzzle to smell the black, churned ground. Once he turned aside to thrash a young holly – its leaves and twigs were sent flying until the torn branches glimmered whitely through the darkness. Buckie and the sorrel stood on the edge of the ground while many does grazed around them, seemingly unconcerned.

The buck stalked toward one, sniffed her white rump and licked it, but she skittered a few steps away with a quiet bleating. He tried again this time laying his head across her back, but still she ran away. The sorrel left Buckie's side and sidled across to the white doe, smelling her and edging up close. Unlike Buckie, he was mature and wild to mate. While the master buck belched and thrashed his antlers, pursuing another doe at the west end of the rutting floor, the sorrel and the white doe slipped around the massive trunk of an oak on the east side. When the sorrel licked her rump the doe ran away, but she only took three steps and bleated to him. Suddenly out of the darkness came the master buck, prancing between them tall and stiff-legged, his groaning fit to split the night and lowering his great antlers. The sorrel did not pause to argue but galloped off down the slope while the master mounted the white doe, belching with triumph.

Some days later, on a still, grey afternoon, Keeper and Shadow splashed across the brook on their way back to Marrowbones. They had been inspecting the butterfly clearings. It was very quiet in the woods with the does drifting away in small, peaceful groups. The rutting fever was over for another year and a chill of winter invaded the twilight air, even though it was only four o'clock. In Amber Great Wood, most of the leaves had fallen now, carpeting over the churned mud of the rutting ground with orange, yellow and sepia colours. Keeper could see great distances up the long slope and the shape of a single beech with its soaring branches and silvery trunk was particularly prominent. Shadow loped along at his side, tired after sending treewards every squirrel in sight. The quick tap-tap of a nuthatch sounded loud in the wood and the air smelled as earthy as beetroot as he tramped through the thick leaves. "A gammon steak for supper," mused Keeper, "with early sprouts from the garden, small as yet, but nutty tasting with…" Abruptly, Shadow sat as she had been taught to do at the sight of deer. Her black nose snuffed forwards, pointing to the left of the track.

Bright colours had faded with the diminishing light and huge grey trees loomed above the brown forest floor. Keeper lifted his binoculars and aligned them along Shadow's muzzle. At first he could see nothing, but a last drifting leaf and then he glimpsed bare twigs? No, they were antlers, and there came into focus, far up the slope, a great buck, slumped between beech and oak, although it was managing to watch them. Its head was up so that he could see the massively palmated antlers

"Good girl. Heel!" he whispered and set off at a slow and steady pace to take a closer look with Shadow's nose close by his knee. The buck watched them approach until they were only a few yards away, then grudgingly, slowly, he scrambled to his feet and shambled away, gaunt and evidently exhausted. Keeper laughed to himself, saying to Shadow, "Should be a good summer for little bucks, I reckon!" then they made for home.

Now that he had been forced to stand up, the master moved stiffly downhill to a grassy clearing, and began to graze as if to make up for lost time. A stocky chestnut pricket followed close behind him. When the fallow deer had begun to drift away from the rutting ground, Buckie had stayed with the big buck, no longer feeling threatened by his huge antlers. He had watched Keeper and his black animal advance up the slope and had slipped away but as darkness fell, had returned to graze beside the big buck. Then, moving ahead of him down to the brook, he paused once or twice as if waiting, looking back over his shoulder, before trotting on along through Ferny Wood. He followed a narrow, familiar deer path through hollies, small oaks and birches, to the ruined cottage. For a while, Buckie haunted the old orchard and garden by night, nosing for cold apples and nipping off the last of the surviving Michaelmas daisies, or sampling the leaves of damson and pear as they drifted down onto the long grass. But each dawn he moved away through the open glades of Ferny.

November brought with it foggy nights. In the chill, early light, scarves of mist hung about bare branches, shredding away as the sun rose, but if Buckie went downhill, the whiteness grew thicker, hanging heaviest and longest over the brook. Along its bank, grass still grew summer-long in the dampness, all lush and juicy. The old buck had settled here ever since the rut, grazing and resting, making up for all the weeks when he had been too racked with passion to bother with mere food. At the wood's edge, bracken had grown to the height of a man by July, but now it stood dry and fox-coloured and was beginning to die down. But it was still high enough to hide him when it was time to rest and chew the cud, so he had trampled down a couch deep among the fern. Buckie had his own smaller one, close by.

One day, as they browsed the last crimson leaves off some elder, Buckie's playmate, the sorrel, wandered down through the wood and splashed across the brook, pausing to graze nearby. When they retired into the bracken, he too made a resting place for himself only a few yards away. Just as Buckie knelt down and then settled his haunches, the wood began to whisper and the twigs to sway. Dead leaves sifted together and a wren cried out 'tic-tic-tic' as two squirrels, squabbling over a buried acorn, bolted for their dreys. From far in the south-west came a huge sighing, then a roar as the squall flung itself at the wood. Huge oaks and beeches threshed and heaved their boughs; somewhere to the east an ancient trunk fell, shaking the ground with a thunderous sound while a million brown leaves raced across the forest floor, as if fleeing a great, invisible giant passing overhead. Then slowly, the wild winds died away and the rains came. That night, Buckie and the others sheltered deep in the pines of

Thorny Knap. All through the dark hours, rain fell in drops big enough to fill a hoof print until ditches ran like streams and hollows turned to pools. Now and then, more violent squalls would tear across the forest, clattering pine branches together and filling the streaming air with flying needles.

Not until morning did the storm die away or the winds sink, then the racing clouds shredded into grey rags, revealing an innocent sky of pale, washed blue. By noon, when the bucks were moving back through Ferny, the sun was shining. The wood steamed faintly in the low, wintry beams, every branch and twig slick and shiny with water and even the light-footed deer sank slightly into the sodden forest floor. As they squelched downhill, a low, rushing roar began to fill the air. Their bracken shelters had been flattened almost to the ground, but the greatest change was in Amber Brook. Instead of a little stream splashing along between mossy banks six feet apart, a torrent of racing, muddy water filled all the bottom of the valley, bearing away twigs, branches, small furry bodies and even a stunted hawthorn on a soupy tide of suds and fallen leaves. For a time, Buckie just stood above it, eyes wide and dark, sniffing at the edge.

Presently, all three ambled back up the slope and settled down under a few seedling pines to chew the cud. The old buck had been slowly building up his emaciated body with good feeding, all to be had within a few yards, so that he had had no need to exert himself. Every night, Buckie and the sorrel wandered off alone, exploring and foraging, but each day they returned here at some time, to graze beside the old master or to couch down in the flattened bracken. Today, as he swallowed his last mouthful, the old one stood up and lifted his head. He sniffed into the wind for a long time, then giving himself a thorough shake, he set out purposefully along Amber Brook, keeping well above the racing water, with Buckie following behind.

The flood had begun to subside now although the stream was still tearing along, churning muddy and deep, but mostly remaining within its banks, although in places lipping the tops. Spatters of bright leaves, orange, brown, green and yellow swept past, caught in eddies of foam. On either side, the banks were strewn with wide puddles between snaking brown roots, undermined by the roaring torrent. Here and there the bank had collapsed and the stream swirled in, claiming a new pool, sweeping away grass and earth, scouring down to the gravel. The deer splashed through shallow puddles but kept away from the main current, eyeing it askance. The old buck seemed to have taken on a new lease of life, leading the younger ones confidently along the edge of Ferny

Wood, leaping across Thorny Gutter into a dark pine plantation. There they paused to graze that night, trotting on upstream the next day to the level heathlands. Buckie often stopped to gaze down into the stream where it foamed over small rapids, or twirled leaves in endless circles in pools free of the main current.

Out on the heath, only a mile from its source, the water of the stream had cleared and once again ran slowly and quietly, although deeper than before. Yet one of the pools was still agitated. The old buck moved past, antlers held high and stately; he had seen it all before but Buckie stopped, peering down at the commotion then stepped back and edged forwards again, to stare down into the water. The sea trout had been waiting for weeks for just such a spate, lurking in dark waters. Now they had swum up through the racing, bubbly currents to this pool to lay their eggs in the loose gravel, the males all agog to spill their milt close beside a laying female, each jostling for a place, so that the pool flashed with silver-green fins, circling and swishing, brushing the small stones and even breaking the surface with a lash of tail.

When Buckie caught up with the old master, he had turned away from the stream. To the north rose a wooded hill, oaks brown and bare now, although pigs still rooted for acorns on the forest floor. To the south stretched the heathland, unburned for years so that the heather brooms grew several feet high. Here the old buck had spent several winters, joined each year by other males. Here they could catch every ray of the low slanting sun, were protected from the coldest winds and there was grazing and a thicket to retreat to in times of danger or serious storms. When Buckie sat down to chew the cud, the brown-stemmed bushes hid him completely.

Others, long ago, had also chosen this sheltered bank; badgers had used it for hundreds of years, their tunnels and chambers extending far back beneath the hill, the bare ground pitted with old entrances, full of drifts of dead leaves. When the sow badger from the Moonham sett had left home, she had wandered all through the Enclosure into Ferny Wood and then headed south to this bank. Prospecting for worms in the damp earth between the bushes, she had found the old sett, empty just then but for a vixen living at the eastern end. So she had dug out a tunnel in the opposite direction, finding, after she had excavated a few feet, a whole labyrinth of passages that were still open. As twilight fell over the wide heath, she climbed up to the mouth of the sett. Staying just inside, she lifted her striped snout to snuff the cold evening air. A new smell of deer hung upon it, but that was not frightening. So out she came, looking around before retreating back down the hole, only to reappear backwards, with a mat of old bracken clasped to her chest, just as Buckie lowered his head for the first evening graze, a mere foot away. Startled, he leapt into the air off all four feet – at once pronking and letting out a single, deep bark of alarm, he galloped out over the heath, bounding over the tall, old ling bushes until he was once more on the bank of the brook, its waters a dull silver in the gathering dusk.

He had just settled down to graze again when another sound made him start up, but this was more distant, and familiar. Two well-grown bucks, one with the light coat of a menil, were splashing across higher up making for the rhododendron bank, their white rumps just visible through the chill darkness. No stars shone tonight but a thin, bitter wind gusting up the valley rustled the dry heather. As Buckie stood, staring after the bucks, something new and strange fell upon his nose. He licked it off – it was very cold and had no taste. It was the first snowflake of winter.

6

White Death

As the sun rose huge and orange in a pale sky, the heath glittered with light, every frond of heather and bracken dusted white with a sprinkle of snow, set hard by a sudden frost before dawn. When Buckie wandered out to graze, he found the grass stiff, tasteless and cold, so he moved on towards the brook. Where runnels drained down into it, water spread out into small pools with patches of bog where tasty plants grew. He had often sloshed through such wet ground, sampling lush mosses, cotton grass and the bog pimpernel's silvery trails of leaves. The going never grew treacherously soft, like the great peat bogs to the east. Now the puddles shone, dazzling as mirrors, the thin ice transparent as glass, reflecting a sky turned palest, cold blue. A bush of old brown heather became a delicate white spray. When he stood on a frozen puddle, the ice broke with a sharp crack and he jumped away, staring back at it sideways. More puddles cracked and he sidled off onto firmer ground and stood with head lowered, staring out over this new, white world before finally trotting back to the rhododendron thicket.

The old buck lay dozing, his body half under the leathery leaves. Half a dozen other bucks had joined them now and the sorrel had moved up into the wood behind, where the great oaks had kept off the frost. Buckie joined them, moving up the slope to graze on bright green moss growing along the north side of a big, fallen branch, the menil wandering across to join him. The forest floor no longer made a mosaic of colour, but was a sea of tawny-brown leaves that gave off a sharp, earthy smell whenever the deer's pointed hooves disturbed them. Later, low sunbeams striped the wood with long, tree shadows and shone back from the scattered hollies glinting on their shiny leaves and scarlet berries.

As the small herd foraged slowly up the hill, Buckie and the menil tagged along. Most of their coats were coarse winter-brown by now, in sharp contrast to their white rumps, shading to greyish flanks and pale bellies. Only the buck highest up the hill was different as his coat was a matt black. With six tines on his tall antlers, he looked proud and splendid, a buck in his prime. Presently he crossed a gravel track and climbed a steep bank to a small clearing sloping to the south. There he sat down to chew his cud, the rest following at intervals, sinking down on the still, soft leaf carpet one by one, Buckie the last to follow. Hardly a twig moved on the still air. In the distance a robin sang out and three blue tits landed on the lowest oak branch and twittered together before flying off. A pale beam of sunlight shone down into the clearing, waking a squirrel who lived in a secure drey in a leaf-lined hole twenty feet up in one of the oldest oaks. He came to his entrance, stretched and peered out, sitting bolt upright and staring out over the wood with his nose working, testing the air. The sun struck coppery tints from his grey fur as he ran his paws across his face several times, like a person trying to wake up. His nose found the air to be safe but cold. He retreated into his hole and huddled down into the soft bedding, curling his tail over his head before going back to sleep.

Down below, jaws were moving slowly and Buckie dozed, secure among the bigger bucks. Three rabbits came to nibble grass along the rise. Then suddenly, a truck came roaring towards them, startling the deer to their feet and rousing a wren to ticking fury. The truck killed one of the rabbits that bolted the wrong way. It stopped just below and men jumped out and stared up through the wood. They pointed and shouted and set off up the hill, billhooks in hand as the deer scattered in all directions, so that the men only glimpsed a few white rumps disappearing through the farthest trees. But it was the trees that they attacked, picking out the hollies with the thickest berry crop, climbing on each other's backs to reach the highest branches and hacking off whole boughs and tops. They gathered them into rough bundles which they secured with twine and loaded them into the back of the truck, still trampling and shouting until all the southern slope lay littered with discarded branches. The hollies stood bereft and misshapen, their green bark torn asunder and their hacked limbs showing chewed white bark. Fallen berries were littered everywhere, bright as beads. The men clambered back into the cab and drove off eastwards, the taint of blue exhaust soon sifting away.

When all became quiet, the deer drifted slowly back, Buckie leading, swinging his head from side to side and sniffing the disturbed air, wary but curious. Here and there, the ground was littered with sprigs of leaves where berry-less twigs had been lopped off. He set about munching them while the rest of the herd wandered down and began to feed again all around him, although the old buck had never moved from his favourite couch under the dark-stemmed rhododendrons.

A pair of crows, flying home to roost, saw the body of the rabbit and sailed down through the chill, twilight air, landing close by. They hopped a few yards with feet together and began to pull the carcase apart, one on either side, tearing at the grey fur. Squawking and stabbing at each other with their cruel black beaks, they raised their wings in threat, snatching and gobbling the red meat that meant survival in the bitter cold. Buckie took little notice, chewing his cud. Blood-smell drifted along the bank. The sow badger, testing the air inside her sett, caught a whiff of it and padded out past the old buck. Climbing up into the wood she went straight to the carcase. The crows swore at her and bounced about stiff-legged, darting their beaks, but she took no notice as she lowered her striped head and began to feed, crunching it up, bones and all. The crows flew off into the dark. They had eaten about half the rabbit and the badger gulped down the rest. Feeding was not easy with the ground frost-hard and she must eat for more than one since her cubs would be born towards the end of February. Meanwhile, Buckie had stood up and stretched, gazing around.

The boar badger had slept on for longer. By the time he ventured out, only a tattered and bloody little rag of rabbit fur remained. He nosed over it with his round black snout before moving on up through the trees, heading away from a small commotion among the dark boles. Buckie, the sorrel and a newly-arrived yearling were chasing each other round and round an old tree stump, bumping their foreheads when they met and shoving shoulders, kicking out their hind legs and pronking over the forest floor.

Every night a white frost fell hard upon the land. At last the master staggered upright, moving a few yards out onto the heath and nosing about under the old heather bushes to find some still-green grass. Though they grew continuously over the years, his teeth had become uneven so that he could only cope with eating grass, while the rest of the herd browsed on mosses, bark stripped straight from a tree, seedling conifers or holly growing at the wood's edge. For chewing their cud, the deer rested in the south-facing clearing in places where it caught the thin winter sun, or they moved down to the thicket, sitting in a loose half-circle around the old buck until the snow began to fall. White flakes spiralled down, softly and slowly at first, drifting like pigeon feathers on the air. Buckie sneezed and blinked when they landed on his long eyelashes – but this was only the beginning. Flakes began to fall faster, whirling down out of a dirty-white sky, covering the ground in a thick blanket.   The whole herd, including the old buck who was now a little stronger, moved up into the densest part of the wood led by the black deer. Even here the bare branches only broke the fall a little; snow still came thickly down, covering the ground and the grazing. They scraped at it with pointed hooves, uncovering perhaps a wisp of grass or single tuft of moss. When the black buck turned westwards, they followed him downhill in a wavering line, Buckie and the other young ones staying together and crossing the gravel track that was now a white ribbon. They entered the sanctuary of Moonham Enclosure, leaving a trail of neat hoof prints and scatters of shining dung.

Here, the close-planted pines had so far kept out most of the snow. They had been brashed that year, their lower branches lopped to encourage tall growth and most of them had been left to die, swagged with dying needles. Now the soft floor and all the brash wore a thin white speckle, lighting the usual brown twilight under the Scots pines. A flock of long-tailed tits were chasing about in the upper branches, their gentle 'kiss-kiss' calls the only sound under the sighing of the trees. Sometimes, the weight of snow became too heavy for a bough and it cracked and fell off, sliding down with a soft thud.

Buckie nosed about, finding an occasional snack of bramble or ivy, but little ever grew here in such deep shade. Soon he was driven to chewing at needles left on the brash. The herd met up with a group of does but they took no notice of them now. Buckie unknowingly wandered past his own mother but when he and the other young ones moved on through the Enclosure, he did recognise familiar ground. They high-stepped over the lopped branches until they came to the western boundary fence and then looked across to the ruined cottage with its white-capped walls beyond the white orchard.

ilvery fieldfares and a few redwings had at last found a few knobby, gnarled crab apples clinging to a tree by Ivy's Lawn while others pecked about in the deep ruts made by Keeper's Landrover. He had been into the town to pick up what stale food he could find. Seeing the desperate birds he stopped and threw out a few rolls, watching the redwings. Like plump thrushes, they had a dab of warm red beneath the wing. He knew they liked fruit best, but the bread might just keep them going for a bit longer. When all was quiet again, Buckie and his little gang ducked under the wire at the familiar scrape and came out onto the grass, scattering the birds. He scrumped up a bread roll – it was strange and dry but at least it was something to eat. The birds soon came back, hungrily pecking up the crumbs. When all was done Buckie and the others moved away through the cold grey air which hardly seemed like daylight, ambling back to the rest of the herd couched under the rhododendrons.

Keeper heated water and soaked more bread and took it into his garden. As he stood there in the glistening whiteness and the terrible cold, a high, eerie scream floated up from Ferny Wood – a fox calling for its mate. The world still turned then and life would go on, but the land seemed locked in a terrible loneliness. He shivered and went indoors. By morning, snow quilted the land and lay in billows almost up to the window ledges. A huge, drifting whiteness blanked out the forest, swirling so thickly that he could hardly make out the shapes of trees in his own orchard. At the north end of the cottage, snow had drifted so deeply that a ramp of it nearly reached the upstairs window and a great billow hung across the corner like a frozen wave, its crest ever about to fall. Keeper boiled more water, soaked more bread and cleared the bird table, knowing that the little birds were the ones most at risk.

The buck herd under the rhododendrons had grown in number now and fifteen of them slithered out that night. Under a cold moon they wandered the heath, but when Buckie went to eat a greenish tuft, it spiked his nose. When the master moved back up the slope into the wood they all followed, pawing frantically at the snow which was only a little thinner under the trees. The vixen, whose screams haunted the night, had moved into the west end of the badgers' sett. Now, not waiting for darkness, she raced out across the ice, a warm glowing shape the colour of autumn beech leaves on the white expanse. She snatched up carrion, her thin face intent and her mouth stuffed with tiny bodies, leaving a trail of bright feathers across the snow.

Back in the thicket, Buckie smelled two things: fresh leaves and human being. Hunger overcame his fear and he ventured up to the edge of the wood. There, Keeper with a long-handled billhook, was reaching up to cut down any holly or ivy he could find – indeed anything green to keep the deer going. Buckie and the younger deer found the food first, but soon all the rest of the bucks were moving about the forest floor, grazing up every leaf. When Keeper went to replenish his bird table next morning, he noticed that the snow–wave had lost its crest at last, although the air seemed just as grey and chill. From the wood came the first spatter of water drops. When Buckie scraped at the snow, it no longer crisped into new shapes, but fell silently away, all sloshy and wet – the thaw had begun.

The pair of badgers in their fox-sheltering sett had not been out for two nights. Smelling the cold outside, they huddled deeper into their bracken beds. Tonight, the boar badger stretched and shambled up the long passage to the surface. Finding the entrance partly blocked with snow, he cleared it with one long-clawed paw, tested the air and then moved out to dig a new latrine pit through all the white stuff. As he squatted over it the sow appeared and soon they moved off together, pausing now and then to push a snout into the snow and gobble up dead birds.

All through the wood, snow began to flump to the ground as the boughs lost their heavy loads. Drifts began to slump away and ooze water, until the brook topped its banks. Buckie and the other young deer burst out onto the forest track and galloped up and down it through the wet, softening stuff. Late in the day, they wandered back to the main herd, snatching at any green tufts in passing, a cushion of moss here or a few bramble leaves there. Soon the whole forest was glossed with water, every small ditch becoming a torrent although the land still lay beneath a cover of snow. Then, as the early January twilight fell, a north-easterly gale sprang up, peeling back the cloud that had covered the sky for so long. Once more stars shone out, and Orion with his three-starred belt hung above Hogshades. A bitter wind blasted through the wood, howling past the tall firs of Malwood and roaring up the slopes of Amber Great Wood through the huge oaks and beeches, freezing everything it touched.

In the morning, a red ball of a sun rose in an eggshell blue sky, but there was not enough warmth in its low-slanted rays to fight the arctic wind. The whole forest glittered and shone, every thinnest twig reflecting light. Never had the land looked so beautiful – or held such danger. That night, the large herd of bucks wandered out onto the frozen heath, nosing hopelessly about before setting off for the white wilderness of Foxmoor. They were led by the oldest buck with Buckie and the younger ones trailing along behind, and when the first light of dawn shivered out over the forest, most of them had converged on the pond. For a time, they searched for grass along its banks, nosing under willow and gorse, trying to scrape through to frozen heather. When the sun rose, the master's shadow lay darkly on the glittering ice of the pond. A pair of

Brent geese who used to live on the island had flown south to the coast, but the mallards remained, three brown females and one emerald-headed drake, their webbed feet slapping disconsolately on the frozen surface. But deep under a yew thicket which had taken over one side of the island, there was still a place where thin ice cracked underfoot and there they could dive for food.

Buckie was pinched with hunger. When he sat down under the birches, there was little cud to chew, so he stood up again and mooned off to chew what sprigs he could find along the pond's edge. Even at noon the sun did little but spill its rays across the heath, patterning the snow with shadows. Towards evening, the oldest buck moved away from the pool and stood alone for a long time, staring out over the white land, then slowly, with his antlers high and tail towards the sun, he set out eastwards. Buckie watched at first and then began to follow, the thin pricket and the sorrel deer trailing along too. A general movement began all around as bucks stood and stretched, watching them go, before beginning to move in the same direction. By nightfall they had joined up again into a compact herd, Buckie keeping close to the leader. They were now at the far end of Foxmoor – country that was strange to him. As Orion swung coldly across the sky, they swerved round to the north into a sheltered dip of land called Slofters. It was generally shunned by deer and cattle for the bog in its bottom was treacherous and deep in normal weather, but now they trotted easily across its hard ground and frozen pools. Soon the land began to rise towards the steep slope of Pine Ridge. Before dawn, the old buck paused so that they could scrape about for moss or bramble. The snow was not so deep here, on the southern side. He found a thick tuft of moss under a wide-spreading beech, between two forks of root and was able to scrape it out where the sun had softened the ice a little. He champed eagerly at the luscious green.

Most of the deer had at least found a snack. It was the other pricket alone who did not bother to forage; he stood for a long time, his head drooping under a cave of holly. A male tawny owl hoo-hooed overhead and far to westwards the female answered, 'kee-wick, kee-wick'. Life was easy for them as the land was littered with small frozen bodies. The pricket seemed to shake for a moment with the effort of keeping upright and then his long legs folded so that he lay sprawled on the frozen snow. Overhead, a night wind sighed through the branches and somewhere close by, two branches scraped together with a dark creaking.

They had soon exhausted what forage there was in the small wood and began to move on upwards, leaving the shelter of the trees for a steep slope of snowy, frozen heather. The old buck led, as usual and the younger ones were last in line. Where the snow had begun to melt but then refroze, the slope was so slippery that even deer hooves slithered about. The thin pricket had struggled upright and emerged from his holly shelter. He struggled on, last of them all, but when his small hooves slid backwards on a particularly steep bank, he staggered and fell again. Buckie was the nearest to him; he looked round, stopped and waited, but this time the pricket made no effort to get up, lying where he had fallen on the icy ground, too weak and tired ever to rise again. Buckie stared back for a moment longer and then trotted on as fast as he could, catching up with the sorrel and then with the rest of the herd as they struggled up the last and steepest slope of Pine Ridge. Even the black buck fell once, sliding backwards for several feet before he could scramble up again. Every deer blew out a cloud of white breath on the freezing air. Buckie and the sorrel were up among the leaders as the ground levelled out and they found themselves on a flat white space, once a forest gravel track, its far side marked by a straggly line of thorn trees and bramble which had caught the full force of the blizzard howling down from the north. Snow had drifted over the stunted trees until they were hidden under a great white comber that reared above their antlers. As they reached the summit one by one, the wind fell. They stood about, steaming faintly under a low dawn sky that was bulgy and grey as an old feather bed. The land lay very still, until a squabbling of crows broke out somewhere down the southern slope, where a cloud of dark birds quarrelled over a skinny deer carcase.

The veteran buck stood with his grizzled muzzle facing north towards the huge snow bank that had been sculpted by the wind into great billows and cornices, with blue-shadowed hollows and gullies. Buckie and half a dozen of the others wandered hungrily along the track, finding hardly a leaf to eat and they soon drifted back again, ice cracking beneath their hooves, to find the rest of the herd moving slowly away. A quarter of a mile eastwards, a gap appeared in the drift that walled them in from the north, where an ancient hawthorn, unable to bear the weight of the snow, had keeled over. The old buck turned off towards it and they all followed slowly, Buckie among the last. The feather-bed sky warmed the land a degree or two, just enough to start the ice melting. Buckie, with his light weight, walked downhill over the snow but the heavier bucks felt the ice begin to crack beneath their hooves, for this northern slope had caught the full weight of the blizzard. Halfway down a circle of snow showed up, pure white, no gorse or heather tops spoiling its shining space. As the old buck walked across it, he sank up to his belly and then even deeper. Long ago, this ridge had been used for wartime bombing practice. Although it had long since grassed over, its shape remained. The old buck struggled in a pit of snow.

Buckie backed away, his eyes big and dark, frightened by the strange movements of head and neck sticking up out of the ground. The buck threshed forwards as if swimming in a solid sea, holding his muzzle high to clear the snow so that his antlers were thrust right back. He began to gain ground and rise, so that his rump pushed through the snow cover, but then he slumped again. With chin held high and eyes rolling, he made a last great forward effort, his front hooves at last finding solid, hard bank. With a last, muscle-rending heave, he floundered up onto level ground, shook himself and then set off down the hill at a trot. Buckie and the rest followed and the snow cover thinned a little as they came down off the heights.

Buckie had almost caught up with the leaders now, when suddenly the old buck fell down dead. As his body settled into the snow, the rest of the herd caught up and then passed by, their momentum leading them on downhill. For a moment, Buckie was at the head of the herd, a faint new, enticing smell tickling his nostrils, but then the big black buck came shouldering through as they reached the foot of the hill. They had a glimpse of buildings through a scatter of trees – and a forest of strange antlers.

Summer grass! They broke into a tired trot and finding an open gateway, pressed into the Deer Sanctuary. Shoving hard between the others, Buckie buried his nose in the soft, golden-brown stuff and ate and ate, while all around him the bucks pressed forward to get at the lovely hay. So the master had not died in vain. Not only had he saved the lives of many deer, he had implanted in Buckie's young brain a memory which might well save him again in bitter winters to come, a memory of incalculable value which he too would pass on one day.

7

Island in the Mist

By February, only tatters of snow remained under north-facing banks and a mild south-westerly wind blew across the forest, yet many deer remained in the sheltered meadows of the Sanctuary. They were no longer fed, but the pastures and hedges provided better feeding than the snow-sick winter grass outside.

In the early February dusk, the black buck suddenly confronted a five-year-old rival. For a time they stared at each other, then lowered their heads and clashed antlers with a sound like clattering walking sticks, each shoving hard. They were well matched and neither gave an inch of ground. Their antlers became interlocked, so that one had to back off in an embarrassed sort of way, shaking his head until the tines were free. With chins almost on the ground, they closed again, this time the black one giving way a couple of feet, so that Buckie, who was watching, had to jump aside. Further along the hedge, a couple of other bucks squared up to each other so that the clatter of antlers sounded far out across the forest. Now the black buck was winning and shoving forwards, yet when they broke apart, neither deer ran away. The five-year-old leapt into the air off all his four hooves and pronked away, stiff-legged, while the black one arched his back and threw his heels in the air like a bucking bronco. Soon they came together again and danced round each other with lowered heads, waving their antlers to and fro. Another pair began bucking and pawing the ground, so that the sound of mock battles sounded through the gathering dusk all around the Sanctuary fields.

Although the big bucks were only play-fighting, with none of the bitter battles of the rutting season, the younger ones kept out of their way and began to form a group of their own. There were half a dozen prickets, a sorrel or two and Buckie. For several nights towards the end of February, they wandered up onto the slope of Pine Ridge, nuzzling among the old heather and gorse for grass or bramble, but each dawn saw them back in the Sanctuary fields. A herd of does kept to themselves in the western meadows until one day, when celandines showed their varnished yellow in the banks, hazel catkins blew in the wind and a blackbird sang from dawn to dusk, Buckie set out. He avoided a main road and a car park and with the rest following him up onto Pine Ridge, they then proceeded down the long slope to the bank of rhododendrons with their dark leaves shining in the weak spring sun, their flowers still scaly green knobs.

Now he turned westwards wandering aimlessly on to reach the next green shoot, until the herd found themselves caught between a road on one side and a bog on the other, the wood having narrowed to a mere straggle of pines. One sorrel struck out to the left through tall old heather brooms, but he was soon floundering in stinking black ooze. When he managed to struggle out again, he was plastered to the belly with dark mud. Several others stood still, gazing back the way they had come but Buckie moved slowly onwards, grabbing a mouthful here and there, though the whole forest was still sodden with thawed snow and February rains. At last, he came to a way out across the bog, a causeway built for walkers. As if he had known it all his life, Buckie turned smartly along it with the little herd following him, tip-tapping across a wooden bridge in the middle, before trotting up onto a small hill.

Since the soil here was sandy, water had drained quickly off its slopes and so the grass was greener. Cross-leaved heath grew here too, its grey-green leaves showing a little colour under the well-spread stands of pine and birch. There were thickets of gorse and bramble here and there as well as dead bracken, broken down earlier by the weight of snow, but still sheltering a little grass beneath. The herd spread out and grazed under the tallest pine and a small, spotted woodpecker bounced across the clearing to work over a fallen branch, its scarlet cap the only bright colour in the winter landscape.

Buckie had found some tasty sprigs of whortleberry, bare of leaves, but still juicy. A small holly had fallen in the winter gales, though enough root remained below ground to keep it alive. Under the cave of its branches, a vixen had dug out a well-hidden den. Below Buckie's questing nose she slept on, curled tight on the bare earth where her cubs would soon be born. Soon he lay down to chew his cud and slowly the rest of the herd joined him, sheltered by a gorse brake. The goldcrest paused in her song to go hunting for spiders. Many of her kind had perished in the great frost, each small corpse providing a mouthful for the searching vixen. At nightfall, Bracken Hill became an island in a mist of sepia-coloured bog, the last grey light shining back from a thousand pools of lying water. But the bucks remained on their sandy hillock and stayed, in fact, until the gales of March rollicked through the trees and the sun lay warm enough on the land to set every twig and leaflet steaming. Below, in her earth, the vixen suckled three blind cubs. Once, a party of birdwatchers crossed the causeway dressed in dull greens. They stood gazing about with binoculars, exclaiming softly at some fancied rarity, but they never once glimpsed the fallow deer.

For all the longer days and warmer air, few plants had put on new leaf as yet. Bracken Hill was only small and by now, the deer had grazed off all the best feed, so one night, when the vixen trotted lightly down the path to a rabbit warren on the lower slopes, Buckie and the rest followed her, branching off to the causeway. March winds had dried out the thick, black ooze but patches of true bog remained, where the cotton grass would presently fly its little white, woolly, warning flags. So the deer spread out over the flat space, nibbling at sphagnum growing round the bog's edges since most of the water lovers, such as bog pimpernel and St. John's wort had hardly resprouted yet. Buckie and the rest wandered on southwards lying up by day near a fast-flowing runnel, where grass greened the bank. Next night, they wandered up a dry, heathery slope, still in its winter browns. Down the other side they found a vast, empty heathland, where grass and heather gave way here and there to long, arid stretches of tarmac and concrete, cracked and broken-edged: a disused airfield.

Although the old ling bushes here were tall enough to hide up in and sheltered grass beneath their wiry stems, it was somehow a threatening place, the sky seeming too vast. Buckie instinctively avoided the old runways. Throughout one cold, bright day the little herd lay up in the heather, while a lark practised his spring song and half a dozen ponies grazed nearby. A flock of chaffinches landed in a gorse bush nearby, twittering and fussing before flitting off with a flash of pale feathers. As the red sun sank westward in a sky of palest, eggshell blue, Buckie stood up, stretched each back leg and began to amble off southwards.

One by one the rest of his gang roused themselves and set off slowly in the same direction. By midnight, they had crossed a familiar land and found the cover of woods where there were well-spaced oaks and beeches. Deer and pigs had long ago gobbled up the acorn crop and the great trees stood bare and wintry still. Although buds thickened on twig ends far above, there was little to eat down below, except snacks of moss. They moved slowly on, snatching a mouthful of green where they could, until brought up short by a fence. It was not an easily negotiable fence of wire strands, but a stout barrier of white, wooden palings, too tall to jump. There was a tang of wood smoke on the air. Buckie nosed along the base of the fence, smelling good grass on the other side. It was set on a low bank that had been holed by rabbits. In one corner a hole had fallen in, leaving a space under the bottom rail. He scraped at the broken bank with his sharp front hooves, put his head to the hole and saw grass on the other side – lots of it and he managed to wriggle through. At once he began to graze while the rest followed, enlarging the hole as they came, settling to feed in the paddock of Marrowbones Lodge.

When lights came on in the cottage, the deer took little notice; there hadn't been feed like this since the Sanctuary. Close by, a pony stamped in its stable but they were too used to ponies to be alarmed. Inside Marrowbones Lodge, Keeper finished a large breakfast and then went out to check the van. In the dim, misty light, he glanced across at the paddock to see if his daughter's ponies were out yet – and swore. A group of young fallow deer were grazing his best grass. Most of them looked slender but strong, with their little pointy antlers and big dark eyes, still in their shabby brown winter coats. They were a beautiful sight just the same, if only they were anywhere else and in a way, they represented the future of the forest. Shadow whimpered to be off. Of course, there were always deer about the environs of the Lodge, usually does, or one doe with a fawn in summer. But none had come into the paddock for a long time, discouraged by the white fence and maybe Shadow's smell about the place. Drawing nearer down the garden path, he could see one particularly fine buck with promising, long, V-shaped antlers. Some of the others had a slightly weedy look but no wonder after such a hard winter. Nevertheless, they could not stay in the paddock eating the ponies' grass.

Keeper stamped along the path, clapping his hands and the deer froze. Heads shot up on their long necks, ears held high and alert. For a moment they stared at him and then they pronked away, startled, galloping to the far corner. They sailed over the fence one by one and vanished into the wood which came right up to his western boundary. A green woodpecker looped across the paddock and a wren set up its 'tick–tick' alarm cry from the garden hedge, a rising sun netting the wood floor with tree shadows. The fallow might never have been there but he feared they would be back.

All day, Buckie and the rest lay up under the oaks, chewing their cud, or sometimes strolling off for a snack of moss. Their brown backs and pale bellies were a perfect camouflage among the drifts of old brown leaves, broken bracken and the grey bark of massive beech boles. Once, a skein of fur shook the bare branches overhead – four squirrels chasing each other, line astern. A pair of crows building a nest nearby landed close to the herd, tossing leaves aside with their black beaks to reach the grubs hidden beneath. A clump of pines at the wood's edge had just become a rookery, the needle floor littered with bird-white and bits of twig. All day, the clamouring and cawing went on as birds flew in with freshly snapped-off twigs or stolen ones from a neighbour's nest. Only as dusk fell did they begin to quieten and settle down. At the same time, Buckie and the herd crept back from the wood and squeezed, one by one, back under the white fence.

Next day, Keeper found the scrape and blocked it up, but the following night Buckie found that he could jump the fence and the rest sailed over after him. Shadow had been trained to sit down at the first whiff of deer which was not too frightening. But one night, the deer found two, snappy little Jack Russell terriers (which Keeper had borrowed) in possession of the fence and they jumped smartly back into the forest, away from the wildly barking pair. But later they returned and, in fact, the skirmishing went on that way all week long. Once, the deer found that the ponies had been locked out of their stable and left in the paddock all night, so they joined them. They were used to ponies everywhere in the forest. When Keeper discovered that the deer had actually broken into his vegetable garden and eaten the last of his sprouts, it was too much. He picked up the telephone.

Early on Friday morning, Buckie was sitting chewing the cud in a glade of the big wood, his back sheltered by a huge chunk of beech bole that had fallen long ago, while the rest of his herd were spread out across the forest floor, drowsing or chewing likewise. A hazy, mild sunshine began to filter through the bare boughs, lighting distant clearings; spring was beginning to stretch and stir through the land. Already, dark green spears of bluebell leaves had thrust up through the old leaf mould and a thrush sang high and clear from an oak bough.

The wood was netted with shadows, sunshine and birdsong. Buckie finished chewing and drowsed off, comfortably full, lulled by familiar sounds: the tap-tap of a nuthatch, a blackbird scuffing about in the old dry leaves making enough noise for six, and the scritch-scratch of squirrel claws.

Down the road, a quarter mile from Marrowbones Lodge, hooves drummed a hollow sound on the ramps of horseboxes and a cattle lorry labelled 'Hounds' drew up beside them. Keeper arrived in his dark green van. When the lorry ramp was let down, a sea of hounds flooded out: large, pale dogs, patched with brown and black. When a man in a green coat blew a small horn, horses and dogs in the first relay, known as tufters, began to move off towards the Lodge. Buckie had smelt horse and heard the clopping of hooves on the road below, without even lifting his ears to the alert position. Such sounds often floated up into the wood as riders took to the forest. Then suddenly, it was all too close. He leapt to his feet, smelling dog and trotted uphill just as the rest of the little herd woke up to this new danger. There was nowhere to hide in this ancient wood with its huge, well-spaced trees. The nearest hound, working until now with his nose, at last sighted Buckie and bounded after him with a deep salvo of barks. Prickets and sorrels raced away, for the dogs and their terrible baying seemed to be everywhere. Squirrels shot up into trees, pigeons flapped up from the high branches, clapping their wings and a wood mouse whipped back under the fallen beech as the ground shook under pounding hooves.

Buckie reached the crest of the hill but still the great dog was close behind and soon more and more of them followed, tainting the air. He galloped at full stretch between bare beech and oak trunks, flying over fallen branches, going right down into the valley, his eyes wide with fright. At Amber Brook, he swerved off into the close-planted trees of a new plantation, the others following, all obeying the fallow deer instinct to circle back. Buckie broke out of the plantation, still trying to follow the brook around, with a sorrel beside him and the leading hound still close behind, its tongue lolling, bright-eyed and tireless. Two green-jacketed riders turned across the wood and cantered back to the car park where they set free the rest of the hounds. Released at last, they rushed down the ramp, bounding with energy, their tails agog in the mild sunny air.

The hounds erupted into Amber, just as Buckie and the rest had circled back almost to the fallen beech. With great keenness, they rushed up the hill to join the tufters, spreading out with deep, joyful barks – it was not often that they

76

hunted a whole herd! Soon, Buckie and the others had been turned eastwards by the hounds and then out onto Stoney Plain. They ran along the foot of Pine Ridge and right across Foxmoor Heath, bare country, where they were always in full view of the hunt. Buckie ran and ran as if he had never done anything else, soaring over bushes, on and on, with the dreadful barking still close behind him and the sound of heavy panting. With a huge effort he made a sudden spurt and galloped off to the right towards a far, misty line of darkness. It meant trees and some sort of cover, but the hounds outflanked him and he was driven on, his eyes bulging with terror. They went past the pool, down towards Furzy Green and on across the lane, where traffic actually stopped, people exclaimed as they watched deer and dogs streaming by.

Buckie was confronted by the steep side of the common just as his legs were beginning to tire. He eyed the thickets of gorse and small stands of birch for shelter but the hounds were too close. They still bounded, tirelessly it seemed, after him and the rest of the herd. He could still hear their panting breath frighteningly close behind him, although they had stopped barking. A few hounds and riders had split off pursuing some of the herd that had broken away, but the rest followed Buckie up onto the level summit. There he gathered what small strength was left and set off westwards. But soon the hounds had also reached the level ground that was flat beneath their pads and with Buckie in full view, they swept after him in full cry once more. Buckie's legs began to ache and even to wobble as, leaping a shallow pit, he staggered. He ran on somehow, his breath coming in harsh snorts as the hounds drew nearer and nearer. He jumped a gorse brake, fell, scrambled up, ran on, every bark seeming like a blow on his small head. Somewhere among the clamour of shouts and barks a horn blew, but Buckie stumbled on and, trying to leap a boulder, he fell – and this time lay still.

Even without a kill, the Buck Hunt had enjoyed their best gallop of the season. Keeper thanked them for their help and reckoned that the rest of his vegetables would be safe now. It took quite a long time for the rest of the herd to realise that they were no longer in danger. Eventually they all slowed down and wandered up onto the ridge. By now, Buckie had stood up and moved on. Soon they had all joined up again and had a short graze, then flopping down on the short turf sheltered by gorse bushes, they began to chew their cud.

8

Duet for Cuckoos

Before the May sun had risen above the pines of Moonham, Buckie trotted out from the darkness of the wood and ducked under the sagging wire fence, going into the paddock by the ruined cottage. He had been alone for some while now and was rested and alert, his ears held tall and his shining, dark eyes peering inquisitively towards the old stable and orchard. He saw another animal scrambling to its feet, something about his own size or smaller, brownish, with a familiar smell. Snuffing the still air, he wandered over towards it, passing a pony lying in the long grass. A thrush sang out from the old cherry tree and a cuckoo called, somewhere deep in Ferny Wood.

The first rays struck down into the paddock, gilding the new foal so that his coat was burnished to bronze, his little tail and mane a creamy gold. Buckie danced up to him and stood and waited and finally, bursting with energy and glee, he gave him a friendly nudge in the shoulder, to start a game. The foal fell down. Buckie waited, nose weaving from side to side, but the creature lay utterly still so he moved away slowly to eat a tuft of grass, turning to give a last look at the animal lying so flat. He sniffed at the mare lying beside it, her open eyes reflecting a pale blue sky and then he ran away up the paddock and jumped the fence onto Ivy's Lawn. In the warm, still air, the old cherry tree clotted with blossom let fall a few pale petals that drifted slowly down, strewing the ground with pink and white. Three petals fell on the back of the badger from the nearby sett, as she ambled home along the copse edge. The bees were waking, zooming from their hole in the hollow trunk and buzzing off towards Ferny Wood, with all its small holly trees in bloom. Everything tasted extra sweet with the sap rising.

The adder, who lived in the old stable by night, had slithered slowly to his morning station by the gate posts. Gradually warming to life, he had summoned enough energy to slough off his old skin and now half his body was already clear of the dry, papery coat. His new skin beneath was a primrose colour with startling black zig-zags. In the copse, Buckie moved on to bark a hazel sapling, disturbing a squirrel who shot up the nearest tall tree and turned, once safe in its first fork, to swear down at him with the hard kissing sound.

All around, the trees of Ivy's Lawn were bursting into tender green leaf, clouded with the white of hawthorn and wayfaring trees. Little birds dashed from hedge to nest in a flash of blue and yellow, with their beaks full of caterpillars. A peacock butterfly alighted on Keeper's sleeve as he gazed down at the dead ponies, the mare's ribs showing through her rough coat like the bars of a cage. All this flush of spring had come too late after the harsh winter to give her enough stamina to give birth.

The trees still kept their perfect spring colours, for the season had come late this year. The uncurling oak leaves still held a touch of amber and silky beech showed a brilliant, fresh green. The birches all around Buckie were fountains of silvery green. Down in the hollow of a half-dead holly, a great tit was building a snug nest, busily flying to and fro from the old pony stable with trails of straw three times its own length. Soon, confronted with a crowd of tiny, gaping beaks, the tit parents were busy snapping up insects. As Buckie moved under an oak tree, something very small touched his wet black nose, making him start back. It was a pale green caterpillar, swinging on a gossamer thread from the branch above. All through the woods they hung from the trees, scarcely swaying in the still, warm air. Before Buckie could so much as lean forward to sniff the new thing, there was a flash of yellow feathers and the caterpillar was gone.

Ferny offered a feasting of new leaves, sweet bark and succulent grass in the open glades, with the fresh flavours of plantain, self-heal and clover in the turf. Nosing through new bracken, its leaves only half uncurled, Buckie came upon a little shining black eye, watching him intently. Once more he backed off, staring at the long-beaked, chestnut-dappled bird; the woodcock never moved from her four roundish eggs. Only as dusk fell and pale moths flew out through the darkening glades, did the male woodcock take to the air above his nest with slow, flapping flight, alternately croaking and uttering a high kiss-kissing call around his chosen territory. Later, as Buckie sat chewing his cud beneath an oak, the darkness vibrated with a strange deep, reeling sound as a passing nightjar, flat-headed as a snake, paused on a bough above. But it did not stay and flew northwards towards the heathery expanse of Foxmoor Heath.

Next morning, under a warm blue sky, the bees flew out early. Soon every holly tree whirred with the hum of insect, drawn to the tiny, white flowers. Unopened buds showed carmine tips, while those already fumbled and pillaged stewed the wood floor with pale stars. Buckie had grazed early on as many new birch leaves as he could reach and now retired to a stand of small pines, a dark patch in Ferny's glory of pale leaf and blossom. Yet even this darkness was lightened – a lovely fragrance drifted on the still air. Among the pines grew a solitary rhododendron, lifting its flowers like yellow lamps in the dimness beneath the needle canopy. A hedge sparrow moved stealthily about its branches searching for spiders; its nest containing two, sky-blue eggs in its horseshoe cup was hidden away in a thorn brake, close by.

When Buckie stood up, stretching each back leg in turn, the dunnock flew back to her nest, disturbing some much larger bird from among the thorns. She seemed unconcerned that the nest now held three eggs, one slightly larger than and duller in colour than the original two. When she flew off again, another large bird, brownish, with a striped breast alighted near the hawthorn. As Buckie wandered out to graze again, a male bird began to call from high in the pine trees, 'Cuckoo, cuckoo.' But the mate of the first bird who had laid the egg at once claimed the territory as his own, calling from a nearby beech, his voice a fraction higher in pitch. The other challenged. For some enchanted time, Ferny Wood rang with the two cuckoo calls, sometimes chiming against each other, sometimes exactly together, or following, 'Cuck-cuckoo!'

'Cuckoo, cuckoo, cuckoo-oo,' rang so loudly through the wood that Keeper ran from his cottage to make sure it was real, this nursery rhyme come true, a duet of cuckoos that lifted his spirits after the death of the mare and her foal.

'Cuckoo, cuckoo.'

Finally, a slate-grey bird flew up from the pine trees and headed away towards Ivy's Lawn and a green quiet flowed back over the woods. The hedge sparrow laid another egg and a squirrel came out of her drey, high in the oak tree. She selected a sunny fork among the new, half-curled leaves and settled down to groom her ears, rubbing her paws hard and repeatedly over head and cheeks, with the urgency of someone already late for an appointment, the sun drawing reddish tints from her flanks.

Buckie lived among Ferny's glades for a while, sampling young beech where the branches dipped low enough, sweet sycamore bark and new grass. By now, tiny woodcock were scrambling through the jungle-high bracken, desperate to keep up with their mother, whilst a row of great tit fledglings perched along a twig of holly waiting to be fed – and the dunnock had hatched a cuckoo. Whenever Buckie rubbed past a bole or ducked under a branch, tufts of old brown winter coat were left behind, so that several second-brood nests were given a cosy, fur lining. For a time, with his summer coat only showing through in patches, Buckie had a shabby, moth-eaten look.

One mild morning enshrouded in light, misty rain, the infant cuckoo squirmed its blind way underneath the last remaining dunnock fledgling, and tipped it over the rim of the nest, just in time to open its gaping maw for a beak full of caterpillars from the hen dunnock.

That evening, as Buckie sat drowsing and chewing his cud under his favourite pines and mist swept in soft, silent veils between oak and beech, Ferny Wood was invaded. He jerked awake, alert to an alien smell and jumped up and peered about, sensing big, blundering bodies through the mist. He let out an alarm bark, sharp as a gunshot and galloped away fast heading northwards, fleeing the strange beasts which looked a bit like cattle but smelled different. The red deer moved slowly through the wood, pausing to browse here and there, but they were restless and stayed on the move. The big, handsome hinds with coats a dark, reddish brown and yellowish rumps, held their heads high as if commanding all the country round about, with none of the quick, nervous movements of the fallow. In the forest, no-one hunted red deer now although once it had been the sport of kings and no other wild creature could match them for size. So they had no fears, stalking majestically through Ferny Wood as placid as cows at this season of the year. But the invasion had unsettled Buckie so that by morning he was back in the old cottage orchard. Not until evening did he once again duck under the fence to make for Ferny Wood but he did not settle in any of its glades where the red deer smell still hung heavily. Only a magpie noticed his passing, flying up with a harsh, rattling cry from beneath the thorn brake where earlier it had gobbled up a dead dunnock nestling.

By early evening, Buckie had reached Amber Brook that was running low and clear. Splashing lightly through the water, he came to the huge oaks and beeches of Amber Great Wood and threw himself onto the grass bank at its edge. He rolled luxuriously, loosening the very last of his tickly old coat and stood up and shook himself. His summer coat, auburn and spotted with white, matched the sun–dappled woodland floor for beauty.

Evening sunshine streamed through the high, heavy canopy wherever a great tree had fallen in the winter gales or blizzards. Little else of any size grew in the wide spaces between the oak and beech. A small herd of does and their offspring, all shining in their bright, new summer coats, were slowly moving eastwards across the wood, pausing for mouthfuls of holly shoots or bramble. The does were heavy-bodied with this year's young. Buckie began to graze nearby, finding mossy tumps between tree roots and he munched his way along them all evening, moving through the quiet wood with only a thrush singing continuously overhead until lengthening shadows merged into dusk and the tawny owl's cry echoed out over the forest, 'Hoo-hoo-hoo'. It floated down past Buckie to hunt urgently for mice along the stream bank, for on the lowest branch of a pollarded oak growing halfway up the slope, two soft, whitish balls of feathers huddled together, softly 'kee-wicking' to be fed.

Buckie stayed with the herd for a while, but one by one the does wandered off alone to find a secluded place to give birth. Each evening, he and the yearlings played together, bumping their foreheads and shoving, prancing in and out of the shadows. Then one morning he trotted out into the early sunshine to find the wood empty of deer, with only a distant cuckoo calling and nuthatches tapping high above. He ambled down to the stream and stood for a moment, gazing into its shining eddies. Cloop-cloop went the current, lapsing over a fallen branch and spinning along a drift of pale petals. As if suddenly coming to a decision, he wheeled about and set off at a smart trot along the bank, past the closely-spaced, pole-thin stems of the plantation to a wide, grassy plain that stretched away on either side. Here, many cattle and ponies were grazing but along the stream bank there grew thickets of thorn, bramble and briar rose for cover. Grey-green willows shone in the early sunshine, their woolly catkins filling the air with flying fluff – a wisp of it stuck to his wet nose, making him sneeze. Where the bank had fallen away, little bays of bog had grown up and here he paused to sample new fronds of sphagnum and bog cotton, his passing filling the air with the warm, spicy tang of bog myrtle as he brushed past the scaly bushes. A dragonfly zig-zagged, gold and black over deep blue spires of bugle.

Rounding a briar of rose clump, he came face to face with another deer, a little smaller than himself, of a pale brown colour with small, single, unbranched antlers. They eyed each other nervously though neither backed away. Buckie sniffed at it – it was not his own kind, but it was too small to be threatening. The roe buck went back to browsing, for wild rose was a favourite food. When Buckie moved on, he came across the doe; she had the same big, black nose, but no antlers. Her twins were still hidden away in the fringe of woodland. Ignoring her, he browsed along until the stream widened out to pond size, here fringed with yellow iris. A coot pottered about the bank, its white, face shield catching the hazy sunshine and a mother mallard swam out from cover with seven ducklings, line astern. But as Buckie leaned towards a succulent patch of green, an Indian war-whoop tore the peaceful air apart, the ducks and coot scattered for cover and Buckie bounded away towards the safety of a gorse thicket. He was startled by something landing on his head so suddenly! Such a thing had never happened before and since no bird of prey ever came near a deer, he was not programmed to look skywards for danger. He was not in the least hurt by the bright, flimsy plastic, only frightened. Then there were shouts and pounding feet, as the boys rushed up to rescue their kite. His only escape was to break from cover and run. As he bounded into view, the children forgot their toy and gave chase. Buckie streaked away up the stream at full gallop, his neat dark hooves never faltering, flying through the air over small obstacles, fallen branches of clumps of bog myrtle. The children probably only wanted to pat him, but he did not know that so he ran on and on, long after the boys had lost interest and gone back to their parents.

Panic had brought him to an unknown stretch of heathland, a place of wiry, overgrown heather bushes and sprawling gorse. With the wind behind him, he did not smell smoke until he had almost blundered into a long line of fire that stretched away in leaping tongues of red and yellow on either side as far as he could see. Eddies of dark smoke burnt his eyes and nostrils, the air dancing with the heat. He backed away just as a gorse bush caught fire and flared up with vicious suddenness and a harsh crackle, like a salvo of guns. That sent him galloping wildly back the way he had come, unseen through the smoke by the line of Forestry workers strung along the bright line of fire, controlling the burning.

Buckie wandered off back towards the wide lawn, finding the stream again, dipping his head for a drink to flush away the alien taste of smoke. The people had gone home now, leaving the lawn a vast quiet space but for the lapwings that threw themselves about the western sky, calling 'peewit, peewit'. In the fading light, water crowfoot shone in pale skeins on the stream and small, shingly beaches showed up as white crescents. Nearby, a little black and white foal left his mother to go for a gallop in the cool evening air. He came across a grassy pit, an old bomb crater, and suddenly found that the momentum of running down one side shot him up the opposite slope with no effort at all. So he turned and tried it again – whoosh! A chestnut colt came flying over to join in. Soon, the two of them were playing the game in opposite directions until they broke off and galloped wildly away, neck and neck, jostling each other and bucking. They reared, pawed the air and then tore back to the crater for another session. Buckie had been watching all this activity, feeling an impulse to run and join them as he sometimes used to play with ponies in the old paddock. But as he advanced cautiously from his cover near the stream, the chestnut foal's mother walked across to see what was happening. Watching her offspring for a moment, she decided to join the game, although at a more stately pace. Now the black and white foal's mother was drawn in too. Buckie lowered his head to graze – there were too many ponies playing now and they were too big.

Morning dawned grey and cloudy and the warblers woke to sing their tiny, rising phrases. Buckie had browsed his way upstream during the night, but now he lay chewing his cud at the wood's edge. Then, smelling human, he retreated into the trees, disturbing a stoat which had been about to attack a rabbit. Quick as a snake, that slip of ginger fur shot under a clump of bramble. Bolt upright, the rabbit smelled dog and stared at a distant Shadow. When her master raised those glasses, the dog knew she must sit down and keep silent, although the end of her tail quivered and the rabbit smell caused a suppressed whimper of excitement deep in her throat. Keeper laid a hand on her head, fondling an ear, shaking with swallowed laughter as he watched a beautiful pricket, his coat a lovely glowing chestnut even on this dull morning.

Buckie had not noticed the man-smell getting any stronger, so he peered out between the branches at some moving, but apparently unthreatening shapes and finally, inquisitive as ever, he nipped up onto a fallen beech tree so that he could see over the bracken. "Nice little feller," Keeper thought. It could well be one of those that ate his sprouts! He was tickled no end at the sight of this young buck mounting his grandstand to watch the watchers, a party of them who were crouched under a bush seeking the Dartford warbler, keenly leaning forward with their binoculars trained. "Must tell the wife about it," Keeper thought, his pleasure in a good specimen in no way influenced by the venison pasty in his satchel. Buckie stretched his long neck, unaware of the man and dog behind him, the damp wind blowing into his nostrils while he stared at several bottoms, clad in green tweed.

When Keeper went across to speak with the bird watchers, Buckie leapt off his tree trunk and bounded away with a flash of white rump, back into the wood, where the air hung still and grey in the glades. Yet overhead, the wind swept through the heavy canopy, clashing the old branches together, or setting one creaking against another. Here he found a herd of bucks that had moved in with one sorrel amongst them. One had a black back and a further dozen were grazing away from him up a green ride, adults in their bright summer coats, their still-growing antlers covered with thick velvet. He watched them for a while as pigeons croo-crooed overhead and then tagged along behind. For several days he stayed among the herd, going to lie down with them and chew cud when they retreated to a secluded glade to rest in deep-litter couches under the widely spaced boughs of a pollarded oak. In its fork, a pair of jays had nested, and he grew used to their harsh squawks, although the young ones had already flown.

But soon he found himself among buildings, noise, cars and people. Scared and about to turn round to seek his homely woods again, he came across a grassy green bank topped with a fence too high to jump. But there was no need, for all seemed quiet here, the grass grew lush and seemed to go on and on. He had just settled to graze when a distant rattle and roar grew louder and louder until he had to leap away from the great noisy thing rushing right past him on the other side of the fence. Soon it happened again, coming from the other way this time, but fading harmlessly into the distance on a rush of air.

After a day of this, Buckie had grown used to the noise and the shaking of the ground beneath his hooves, the disturbance of air and the alien smell. So he began to wander on along the railway line, retiring by day into a thin fringe of wood to chew his cud before continuing on eastwards. Then he came to a bridge and walked over it with a trit-trot as his hooves suddenly hit the hard surface, lured by the promise of thicker woods on the other side. Some days later, he emerged again onto the bank, having lost his small first antlers, although the empty sockets were already healing. For a time the good grass continued and then he came to a wet, sticky patch which had no plants at all but was just a sea of black, churned mud with an unfamiliar, rank smell, although it was not large enough for a fallow deer rutting ground. Beyond it, grass gave way to sedges and rushes with tough, sharp stems, so he turned away and began to move up through the forest. Ladylands was a vast stretch of mixed woodland, divided into roughly square blocks by gravel rides. Coming across one of these, he followed it to a cottage with a picket fence that was not very high. Smelling fruit, Buckie jumped over – into the garden.

He nosed about in the long grass, munching up all the fallen fruit he could find before turning his attention to the trees, stretching up his long neck – but the nearest apple was still out of reach. So he reared up, his front hooves on the trunk and thrust his head among the leaves. Instantly, a wild, high ringing assaulted his ears and he jumped back, cleared the fence and was away at a gallop along the ride. When all seemed quiet, he had a rest in a beech wood. The long-experienced Keeper of Ladylands had saved many a good apple over the years by hanging a chime of harness bells hidden away in the branches of his orchard.

9

An ill wind

It took Buckie some weeks, moving mostly by night, to reach the familiar territory of Foxmoor Heath and the pond. Here he turned southwards to Cuckoo Copse and the ruined cottage. Nearby, Ferny Wood was all agog for earlier, a cattle lorry had stopped there. When the ramp had reached the ground, three sows trundled blithely down it followed by a dozen romping piglets. Snouts to the earth, they snuffled a few yards along the track and then swerved off into Amber Great Wood, where sweet chestnuts were dropping their first yellow leaves and the leaf carpet lay speckled with golden autumn sunshine as it shone through the thinning canopy. Here and there, an ancient yew tree patched the wood with darkness. When all seemed quiet, Buckie wandered into Ferny Wood.

High up on the slope, a squirrel busily dug a hole between the roots of a beech, dropped in an acorn from her mouth and patted it all down again with both paws, working as fast and urgently as if her life depended on it. She had just started another hole but then shot away, swearing, straight up the nearest trunk, for the gang of piglets had rollicked into the clearing. They had been let loose to mop up the surplus acorns, but for the first hour they were simply drunk with freedom.

Buckie had found a grove of crab apple trees and was busily crunching up the small reddening fruit — there were no bells here! Once he lifted his head to stare up the slope at some movement, but recognising only harmless pig smell on the air, he went back to rooting out the fallen fruit. But when several little ginger Tamworths shot out of the fern almost under his hooves, galloping in tight circles and squabbling over a single acorn, he moved slowly away, ambling north-eastwards to a patch of sunlight. Here, sitting down against the fissured bark of an old oak, he chewed his cud, but not for long. He was still restless and had soon wandered away from Ferny Wood again. All through September, he ranged northwards over Pine Ridge and Mouse Barn to the young trees of White Plantation, joining a big buck for a time, but soon leaving him again, wandering in a wide circle. His dark winter coat had already begun to mar his summer splendour and recently, he had enjoyed a long, luxurious wallow on a riverbank, so that his neck and flanks were still dark with drying mud. In place of the short straight spikes he had carried as a pricket, his newly grown set of antlers was slightly branched, but the narrow beams betrayed the fact that he was still a young animal. It would be another four years or more before he would grow his biggest set and show the wide palmations befitting of a master fallow buck.

As the day drew on, the sows and piglets settled to the serious business of snouting out acorns. By the time the wood pigeons had come flapping down into the canopy to roost, Buckie had reached the high edge of Kings Oak and had paused to swing his small antlers at a ten-foot high holly, slashing into it right and left. The twigs flew and the green bark showed ragged white gashes in the gathering twilight. Out of nowhere, three does came galloping at full stretch, passing him without a glance, heading urgently westwards. He watched their white rumps fade away but made no move to follow. Then far away to the south as the first stars shone out, a guttural, coughing roar echoed out over the forest. Buckie lifted his head and then set off into the tall Douglas firs of Malwood. Here he met up with another buck, his harsh, musky smell overlaying the resinous scent of the wood. Does flitted down the long aisles in small groups, and a buck bellowed out close by. The stars were disappearing one by one as a blanket of low cloud swept up from the sea, a damp wind soughing and sighing through the lofty branches. Soon rain began to fall, silvering the needle canopy. Buckie had chased a group of does a short way and joined up with two other young bucks. Leaving them, he chased a single doe, thrashing a fallen branch with his antlers, aimless, but excited. Now rain fell more heavily until the soaked upper branches could hold no more and dripped heavy gobbets of water. The does vanished away. Buckie and the rest cooled off; they grazed the odd mouthful of moss or fallen twig while the rain hissed down faster still.

For three days and nights it fell, from cloud so grey and heavy-hanging that the days were little lighter than the night. Deep in Malwood, time became a perpetual wet gloom and even the squirrels stayed in their dreys, but the badgers padded out regardless. Buckie took no notice of them wandering past. Two pairs were now living at opposite ends of the great Moonham sett. All four wandered up through Malwood, their white, striped heads the only moving thing in all the gloom, eager for the feast of worms brought up close to the surface by all the rain – until the fourth dawn sent them scurrying for their tunnel's comforting darkness. The cloud had stripped away, revealing a sky of brilliant blue and a gold sun that shafted down into every clearing, gilding every wet leaf and twig, so that the whole forest glittered and shone, every frond and needle reflecting sparks of light.

Buckie stood in a ride, staring down at the sodden gravel and swung his head to and fro, sniffing and smelling nothing strange. But he took a step backwards just the same, since the earth seemed to move as the sun grew warmer. The land had begun to steam gently; wisps of white vapour eddied around Buckie's hooves so he tossed his antlers and set off down the track, which soon became walled by timber. Great stacks of logs stretched away for hundreds of yards on either side; it was cordwood for the Commoners of the forest. The rinsed air smelled clean and resinous.

Where Buckie turned off the track, the sun filtered through the woodland edge onto strange, new, bright shapes; scarlet sickener fungus and purple and yellow russulas. Pausing to browse some moss, he peered at another new shape, a cluster of saffron milk caps. When he nosed them, they bled milky drops of a sinister green colour that smelled odd, so he moved on down towards the ruined cottage. A group of does broke out of the old orchard and streamed away. He raced after them as a breeze sprang up, whipping a few last leaves across the track. As shadows began to lengthen, he came to the outskirts of Swines and met up with a pricket. Another group of does appeared and trotted up, milling about, licking each other's ears and taking a few mouthfuls of grass. They stretched their necks as a belching roar rent the twilight from halfway up the long slope. A tall buck materialised out of the dusk, stared into the distance and swung majestically past into the oaks. The pricket, does and Buckie all followed him up through the huge old trees, under the widespread branches.

Their small hooves threaded narrow paths, already deep trodden and muddy. Many such paths led into Swines from all directions, a spider's web of trails, leading to a dark centre. The rutting floor was a sea of churned, black mud, where the air was heavy with musk even though a gale had begun to roar through the higher branches. At the far end stood a great buck, with tall, widely-palmated antlers. Lifting his head, he let out a belching roar and a newly-arrived buck trotted over to his side. The stared at each other through the darkness and then stalked across the mud, side by side, while more does trotted softly along the ancient pathways and teetered about on the edge. Buckie fidgeted about among them, watching the parading and fighting, deeply excited. Several other bucks, the same age as him or a year older, jostled about near the does. The three-quarter moon, rising over Swines, gleamed on eye or antler or eager wet nose. Once, when the master buck was mounting another doe, Buckie went after one himself, but she ran away into the trees and would not stand for him. Some does were not yet quite in season and most had eyes only for the master. As he paraded up and down, Buckie chased one doe after another, but they all ran away. But in the quiet of the night, one did stand still, allowing him to sniff her white rump to show that she was ready. But almost immediately, another young buck about his own age came prancing up. For a moment they stared at each other before lowering their heads and clashing their small antlers. At the first sound, however, the big buck came charging across, scattering does and prickets alike. For a moment, the huge antlers towered over Buckie before he fled far into the depths of the wood. Behind him the night was rent with victorious roars of conquest.

Buckie mooched along for a while, thrashing another holly bush in frustration. Other deer, in ones and twos wandered around him, their presence betrayed by a gleam of green eyes or a patch of pale rump fur, but in spite of the fright he had suffered, he was irresistibly drawn back to the scene of excitement. The wind had surged to storm force, whipping the canopy into a continual, seething roar. Branches clacked together and somewhere close one fell with a thump. He found the does milling about, agitated by the storm. Just as he regained the rutting floor, the wind howled down on the forest with terrible force and a whole tree fell close by, with a huge noise of cracking and splitting. Buckie leapt away, scared, into a gang of does and yearlings, a wild confusion of bodies in the whipping, howling darkness.

But the master never left his place, stalking up and down the trampled floor and adding his belching roar to the sea of noise. Not far away another giant beech fell, making the earth rumble beneath his hooves. Some high branches broke off with a noise like snapping bones, and still the hurricane howled through the forest. Yet the force within Buckie was as powerful as the storm.

Buffeted sideways, hurled once to his knees, he began to fight his way back up the hill as clouds of leaves and torn-off twigs streamed past him, back to the rutting floor. He could not see the big buck in the swirling darkness but he could smell his pungent reek, close by at the side of the tangle of fallen branches. Buckie began to make his way through the tangle, using his nose to probe ahead in the chaotic darkness, ducking, clambering and crawling but not daring to jump until he reached the other side of the rutting floor. Here many does circled about, bleating and bewildered, but he found one which would stand for him while the master blared on, oblivious, on the other side. Triumphantly, Buckie briefly mounted her but the master buck returned and she broke away.

The storm blew up again, howling down like some huge, demented animal, the wind speeding at a hundred miles an hour off the sea – a death blow. With a tremendous cracking and heaving, rending and splintering, the tallest beech in Amber Great Wood crashed down with an earth-shaking thunder right across the rutting floor. The deer streamed away, whipped by long twigs, but most escaping the heavy boughs that spread far across the woodland floor.

In the first cold light of dawn, Keeper surveyed his forest, and wept to see majestic trees, hundreds of years old, lying prone and shattered, although for Buckie it had been the most magical night of his life.

Tailpiece

Of the New Forest keepers that helped me with deer watching, one lives in a solitary cottage, completely ringed by thick forest. Yet in autumn when word gets out that the red deer rut is on, he has several cars, many from Southampton, queuing up outside. So, although the herd seems to have chosen a really private and secluded place for the climax of their year and only a few walkers will venture that far, the deer are actually being watched through countless pairs of binoculars.

Fallow deer are shyer than the red (and the little roe are even more nervous). So, to ensure the privacy of Buckie and the others, I have moved places about. Buckie's New Forest is not geographically correct. I did want to use the evocative New Forest place names such as Amber Great Wood, Slufters, Skythorns and Marrowbones but have either moved them about, or altered them slightly.

Opinions differ as to how long Buckie's forebears have lived in Britain's woodlands. Were they a native species wiped out by the last Ice Age and reintroduced by the Romans or Normans?

As I write (December 2003), it has been a bad few months for wildlife. The dry summer's end and the early autumn have meant poor grazing at a time when animals need to fatten up to face the rigours of winter. Let us hope that the rains arrived in time to encourage a flush of new grass to get Buckie through the winter.

Apart from the uncertainties of the weather, traffic will remain one of the chief dangers of his life, although he has already shown a certain amount of road sense by making his way safely around Brockenhurst and twice crossing a busy main road. Mortality from any source is always highest in the early years. Now that Buckie has survived these, there seems to be no reason why he should not wander his enchanted glades for many years to come.

Glossary

Black	A dark colour variant of fallow deer.
Brashing	The removal of lower, often dead, branches to encourage tall, straight growth of a tree and circulation of air.
Common	A colour variant of fallow with chestnut coat and white spots in summer, and a black stripe down the tail.
Cull	Periodic killing of surplus deer to keep them in manageable numbers, the old, sick or lame being taken out first by expert marksmen.
High seat	Permanent small platform up a tree with ladder attached, erected where deer gather or pass. Here a census may be taken or a cull carried out.
Menil	A colour variant of fallow deer with a light brown coat and prominent white spots that fade only slightly in winter. No black on tail.
Palmated	A flattening of the antler bone visible in older deer.
Pannage	A New Forest Commoner's rights to release pigs into the forest to mop up surplus acorns that could otherwise cause illness in ponies.
Pricket	A deer older than a yearling, but not yet two years old.
Pronking	A deer bouncing, stiff-legged, off the ground on all four legs at once.
Tines	Spikes on an antler that reveal a buck's age.
Tufters	Hounds kept in reserve to finish off a deer hunt after the quarry has been exhausted by the initial pursuit. (The New Forest Buck Hunt is now disbanded).
Velvet	The thin, furry covering on newly-emerged antlers, later scraped off.
White	A colour variant of fallow with a ginger coat as a fawn and a white coat as an adult, but not the same as an albino.
Yearling	A year old deer with small, unbranched antlers.